MY THOUSAND MILE JOURNEY
ON THE GREENBRIER RIVER TRAIL

DENNY BARKER

To Allen
Allen words can't express how grateful I am of your kind generosity. Going to get that camp built this Summer. You will love it. With all my love

Kathy Barber

Proverbs 3:5B

Copyright © 2019 Denny Barker

All rights Reserved

ISBN-13:978-1-0908-4507-8

DEDICATION

This book is dedicated to the memory of two very special individuals, my Father, Denver L Barker, and my dearest young friend, Brady Powers Mickey. This entire book is written with my dad in mind and Brady, who in the few months we spent together, changed my life forever. Thanks to his wonderful family who supports my endeavor as we continue to carry on in Brady's memory.

ACKNOWLEDGEMENTS

Thanks to Wanda Lester for your help in taxiing me back and forth while I was doing my "Thousand Mile Journey" because without your help this journey could not have been completed.

Thanks to Michelle Barker Wright, Amanda Barker, Mary Lohmeyer, and George Lynch for taking time to read my manuscript and giving me valuable advice, opinions and your tireless effort to edit my vision into a book.

Thanks to Simon Sinek for your inspiration and valuable leadership lessons that have become a cornerstone of future aspirations.

Thanks to Henry David Thoreau for writing "Walden". Walden is my favorite book and a very big inspiration for my book.

Thanks to Richard Adams for taking the picture that was used for the cover.

Most of all I would like to thank my family that has continued to stand by me even when it looked like there was no hope for me. Thanks to all of those that have believed in me throughout these many years and have invested time and money into projects that I have continually worked on. Not one of you has been or ever will be forgotten and as this vision becomes a reality you will each be rewarded.

I would also like to thank the Greenbrier County Public Library in Lewisburg, WV. This entire book was written inside of that library and on public computers. Thanks so much to the Director and the entire staff for their support and assistance.

TABLE OF CONTENTS

PREFACE   Page …1
1. Chapter One   Page …7
2. Chapter Two   Page…21
3. Chapter Three   Page…50
4. Chapter Four   Page…78
5. Chapter Five   Page.111
6. Chapter Six   Page.137
7. Chapter Seven   Page.154
8. Chapter Eight   Page.178

PREFACE

It was June 24, 2018 and I had just finished the exhausting and heart wrenching 2nd anniversary of my father's passing. I had finally settled with the very tragic events that led up to his passing and all the details that went with it. I was, however, struggling with how to continue with my inspired vision and extreme passion that I have been working on for over 15 years. I believe that a previous calling from God several years had set me on a path that I must follow. The passing of my father had interrupted those efforts but over the past few months God had set me back on course. The defining moment that put me back on track happened on November 9th of the previous year. It was my mother's birthday. I never once missed thinking about her on that day. She passed away on September 1, 2003 due to complications from a stroke.

I was sitting in the living room of my father's home that I was in the process of repairing after the flood of June 23-24, 2016. As usual, I was in tears. I happened to be sitting in the exact spot where my mother's hospital bed had been placed during the last couple months that she lived. I was the one that found my father that morning of the 24th. I looked over to the exact spot where I found him that morning and it was only about 10 feet from the exact spot where my mother had passed away. At that moment, the tears stopped and it was as if someone else in the room was speaking. It was so clear to me. The voice said, "You need to quit worrying about your father.

I am now taking care of him. Your father is with me. It's time for you to get back to work." From that moment on I have been able to focus on the task in front of me. My entire focus changed at that time and I started working where I had left off a little over a year earlier.

If you wanted to take the past 15 years of my life and tried to put those years into context, I'm not sure you could do it. Those years still confuse me to this day. There was not a shadow of a doubt in my mind that God called me to do something, but what? I wandered in so many different directions that I couldn't even keep up with things. You see, I was born with a real handicap. I am a true entrepreneur. I am an inventor inside and out. My mind never stops working and I very seldom settle on a single project. Even after that night on November 9th I still could not completely focus on a true direction. Something had to change. That change came on June 24, 2018.

One of the things I truly believe in is that when God calls you to do something you must do it. I was always trying to do what God called me to do. I never doubted the calling and I never doubted my desire to comply with His will. The one thing that most people don't understand is that when God calls you to do something, He doesn't send the calling with an instruction manual. It's not laid out in one-two-three steps and you're finished. You must pray and work for it. You make miss-steps and wrong turns but He seems to know how to put you back on course. I know in my case I would always go way too fast. I always wanted to do things in my time. Several times in my life I would have to stop and take time to pray, fast and do the things that would help me to understand what God wanted me to do.

Notice that dates are very important to me. When you remember the date that something happened it will always be more real to you! June 23-24, 2018 was one of those defining times. I talked to my sisters on social media several times on those days. The bond of grief and sadness is always better shared with loved ones. We all had a very hard time during those days and I spent the time praying and really asking God what I should do. I felt like I had been such a failure in His eyes because nothing was getting accomplished. Well, in my mind nothing was getting accomplished!

In those few days God revealed to me that I was doing everything He expected me to do. I had done years of research. I had invented needed products. Unbeknownst to me, I had completed an entire business plan that could change the world. The plan would change the world for good and in a way that would be very pleasing to God. What I came to realize in those few days was that the entire plan was not possible until now. The country wasn't ready for this change until now. It was not until those two days that everything came together for me. It was like someone turned the light on and I could see clearer than ever. Those that have known me for the past 15 years always knew that I was working on this and never questioned my passion. That was all I ever talked about to anyone. The problem was that I could never explain it to anyone. Folks couldn't figure out what I was doing; was I building furniture, gardens, boats, stabilizers or houses? How was I going to sell these things and how was I going to finance everything?

Many have followed me and helped me along the way. A few years ago, some great friends and family bought cutting boards from me and that really helped. By the way, you all are not forgotten. As a matter a fact, anyone that has helped me is in with me all the way.

The plan was finally coming together. Most of those that have known me for any length of time know that something is different now. My attitude and demeanor have changed. I'm extremely happy now and very sure of myself. Being in the center of God's will makes all the difference.

Here's what I figured out: It has become very clear to me how I am going to get the word out about this plan. I can't take 15 years to do it. I want to turn the light on for other people. How can I make it very simple for them? I will write it all in a book. Wow, that sounds easy! I'm not a writer and as a matter a fact, I'm a terrible writer. Then it hit me: Take the time to formulate it all in your head in an orderly fashion.

I was not in the best physical condition. I was quite a bit overweight and had just turned 65 years old on April 1st. In my entire life, I could never lose weight or get into shape unless I worked out in the extreme, so that's what I decided to do. On July 1st, I went to a flea market and bought a bicycle. It had to be a certain bike with no gears or hand brakes. It needed to be just an old fashioned Huffy 26" boy's bike. Now for the crazy part of this plan! I'm going to ride 1,000 miles on the Greenbrier River Trail in West Virginia. Actually, I decided to ride 922 miles and walk the last 78 miles. This would be quite an undertaking for someone my age and weight, but I felt like this is the only way I could really wrap my mind around this whole thing and present it to people in a way they could embrace.

The idea came from one of my favorite books. A few years ago, a person I worked with at Tracker Marine gave me a book by Henry David Thoreau entitled "Walden". "Walden" quickly became my favorite book. Mr. Thoreau had just graduated from Harvard and wanted some time to determine his future and his mission in life. He took two years to go into the woods and build a cabin on Walden Pond. In the book he records everything. I won't take the time to review his book, but if you are so inclined, you should read it. The one thing I do want you to understand is that although Mr. Thoreau wrote it about the two years he spent at Walden Pond, it was about much more. My book is about more than the 1,000 miles that I accomplished in seven weeks; it's a roadmap to this divine business and organizational vision. It explains how it started, how it progressed and how it will go forward.

My journey was not attempted to just tell this story. It was set up so that every section of the journey was a time for me to concentrate on preset parts of my journey. The first week I would concentrate on my beginning, just like the beginning of the journey. The second week I would concentrate on the part of my story that related to the second week. Fortunately, the 1,000-mile journey was accomplished in seven weeks. That includes a one week break to spend time with family. This total adventure, unlike most of my life, was well planned and could not have worked out better.

One thing I hope you have noticed about this book is that I do not share names. The book is about the experiences and lessons that I learned which brought me to this present-day evaluation and why I am now, at this age in life, attempting to make such a powerful impact on society. Please understand that I do not claim to be a great writer and I will never be a Henry David Thoreau but this comes from my heart and soul. I have invested much of my life into this endeavor. Time, money, sleepless nights and all my passion has been immersed into what I believe God has truly called me to do.

Denny Barker

MY THOUSAND MILE JOURNEY

CHAPTER I
FIRST WEEK - THE BEGINNING

On July 8, 2016, I traveled to Pence Springs, West Virginia to a flea market. The only time they have the market is on Sunday morning and it closes at noon. I was looking for only one thing: a 26-inch bicycle of the old style. I specifically wanted a Huffy boy's bike. I didn't want any gears or hand brakes. It had to be just a simple bike. I had looked everywhere I could think of for such a bike. I even looked on the Internet to see if anyone still made that type of bike. No luck! One of my neighbors told me about this flea market, so I thought I would give it a try. I squeezed in a trip to the market that Sunday morning before I went to watch the final round of the Greenbrier Classic Golf Tournament. I arrived, parked my car, and headed over to see if I could find a bike. As I walked through the many exhibitors, I was only focused on that one thing. As I walked, I looked over about three rows and there it was! I was familiar with that bike because growing up it was the bike of choice. My family had a camp on the Greenbrier River Trail for 40 years and having a bike was very important. I made a quick trot over to the vendor and was amazed at the quality of the bike. It was exactly what I was looking for and it looked like new. I asked the lady how much they wanted for it. I didn't have much cash and hoped that I could afford it. She said the owner wasn't there at the time, but he had told her that the price was $40. I had a total of $45 in my pocket and it was like that bike had my name on it. Without hesitation I gave her the $40 and was on my way back to my car. I named my new bike "Jenny Lynn" after my oldest daughter.

    I had a plan for this bike that I had been working on for a few weeks. As I said earlier, my family had a camp on the Greenbrier River Trail in Renick, West Virginia. When my parents bought the camp from my uncle there was no Greenbrier River Trail. The railroad still made runs through there once a day. My uncle made my father a great deal on a part of the property that he owned. It came with a small house trailer. I was just getting out of college and felt like we were the richest people on earth! Only certain people owned property right on the Greenbrier River! Much of this book will be dedicated to the love I have for this place and how much of my life was built on this small piece of property.

    I had recently turned 65 years old and was at another crossroad in my life. There were two goals that were constantly on my mind. The first was that I had been working on a business plan for about 15 years and really wanted to get that plan out to the public. The other was that I was looking forward to a new grandchild. I had spent some time hiking with my two daughters and two grandchildren and I did ok but was not up to my standards. So, I made the decision that I would work on my conditioning and the plan God had for me at the same time. I had found the perfect bike and it was time to get started. I would start on a 1,000-mile journey on the Greenbrier River Trail. It could only be attempted on that specific trail because it was one of the loves of my life. I would do 922 miles on my bike and would walk the last 78 miles to make the total 1,000 miles. Also, while riding and walking this trail I would focus on this business plan and put it all into words in book form; two things I had never done. Covering a thousand miles in a short period of time and writing a book were both outside of my comfort zone.

    I spent many hours in prayer about this journey. You see, I believe that this business plan was inspired by God and I would really need His help to accomplish this extreme goal. I always stayed in good condition and was feeling well but I had not been on a bike for about ten years, so I didn't have any idea how long this would take.

    During each week of the journey I would focus on a different aspect of this passion. Ideally, if I could do this in seven weeks, it would match with what I really wanted to cover. One of those weeks would be off the trail because my three wonderful sisters were planning a few days with me to spend some much- needed family time. The actual journey had to be done in six weeks. That would mean that I had to average about 167 miles a week and close to one week would

MY THOUSAND MILE JOURNEY

be spent walking the entire trail. I am sure that I will repeat some details throughout the book, but the total length of the trail is 78 miles one way.

I started the journey on July 15th and was able to do 20 miles. I also spent some of the day fishing the river above the Rorer Tunnel. This was always one of my favorite fishing spots. I really had a great day because I caught several smallmouth bass. I must tell you; however, my legs were very tired when I got back to Renick. The journey had begun! The next couple of days I didn't ride very many miles but on the 18th I rode 26 miles, one of the highest totals I had ever ridden in one day on the trail. On Friday the 20th I increased that total to 32 miles. I was amazed at how quickly I settled into a hunger for time to ride. A friend of mine had taken me to Marlinton and dropped me off and I rode back to my camp in Renick. This is some of the most beautiful scenery in the world. I was amazed at how riding in such a beautiful place put me in the frame of mind to focus intently on my plan. Each day, when I returned to my camp, I would write in my notebook of the events and thoughts during the ride. (On a side note: I really got into riding trails and after moving to Williamsburg, Virginia in 2004, I continued to ride. I rode lots of miles but one of the problems I ran into was that I would get bored. Riding sometimes took several hours and your mind wanders. I got so bored that I would count the number of pumps I made in order to ride a mile.) Within the first week of this journey, I soon found out that the time spent riding in such deep thought made time go by quickly and boredom vanished.

MY THOUSAND MILE JOURNEY

On my first week of riding I was able to do 102 miles. I had started posting updates of the miles traveled per day and the weekly totals on my Facebook page. Over time, I developed a very good following of family and friends. I can never give enough credit to those people that supported me through this journey for all their help. I could not have done it without them!

I started out this journey in very good shape and frame of mind but a little less than the average that I would need to maintain. This is much like the way my life started out. I was born in a little town in West Virginia named Marfrance. Marfrance was a little mining town in western Greenbrier County, West Virginia. I was one of five children born to a coal miner father and a truly God-fearing mother. I was born at home in an area called Francis Hill. All of us were born at home except one sister.

When I was two, my family moved to the house that I grew up in: it was about a mile from the house where I was born. I started school at Marfrance Grade School. It was a little three-room school at that time. 1st and 2nd grades were in one room, 3rd and 4th grades were in another room, and 5th and 6th grades were in yet another room. After the third grade Marfrance Grade school became a two-room school. I spent the last three years at that school with the 4th, 5th and 6th grades all together. I really loved going to that school because I had great teachers and so many wonderful friends. By today's standards it was a very poor area, but we didn't know that. Every family was in about the same financial condition and we were very happy. There were lots of families in the area and we never had to search for something to do. We went to school and if we weren't in school or doing chores, we were outside playing from daybreak until dark. Church was at the center of our lives from the earliest that I can remember and throughout my entire life at home. My parents always made sure that we were in church any time the doors were open. We had nightly devotions and I can remember my mother praying until the wee hours of the morning. When a Billy Graham Crusade was on television we would sit and watch with the same reverence as if we were in church.

    We were a very close family then and we still are today. We grew up in two groups. There were two years between each of the older three siblings and four years between the third child and me. There were only two years between me and my baby sister.

    My dad worked very hard in the mines and my mother worked part-time at the school and at Murphy's department store in Rainelle. She then became a cook at my next school, Crichton. Crichton was a 12-year school and I started there in the 7th grade. I went to that school with my next older sister who was still in high school and my baby sister who was in the 5th grade. This was not a difficult transition because my older brother and an older sister had graduated from Crichton and we went to many sporting events there. My brother played football, one sister was in the band and one other sister was a cheerleader.

Much of our lives evolved around our local school. Mom cooked at the school and I was very proud of her and happy that she was there. I remember that one summer I raised a pig and mom furnished most of the feed from leftovers from the school. That pig grew quickly and was very healthy. I was raising the pig for a class at school and the teacher and some of the other students helped my father and I butcher it. My great-aunt and great-uncle made the sausage and cured the ham. The meat was delicious! So much of our early life was built around extended family and we were so blessed to have them.

The real change in my life came after my freshman year. I began my sophomore year at a new school. For the first time I became aware of the term consolidated. Greenbrier County was divided into two sections. Greenbrier West and Greenbrier East and the four high schools in our area were combined in a new facility in Charmco, West Virginia. I played football at Crichton in junior high and now I would be playing at a much bigger school, so I went early to the new campus. We started practice on August 1st. Now I was playing with most of the guys that I usually played against! I had a hard time the first year due to complications with my tonsils and missed quite a bit of school, but I settled in by my junior year. I became a better football player and then went out for wrestling. I had never heard of scholastic wrestling. I was only familiar with the fake "rasslin" on television. I wrestled in first match I ever saw. I was so nervous! In team sports, there are other people around you who are competing but in wrestling it's just you. My father very seldom got to see me because he worked the evening shift, but my mother was at most of my home matches and football games. My older brother was also a great supporter.

    My senior year was my best year. I had lost much of that baby fat that always hindered me and became a more conditioned athlete. I made the All-Southern Team in football and went to the state competition in wrestling. I will remember one certain wrestling match forever. As I said earlier, my father never got to see me wrestle because he was always working but this day, he was off. I was undefeated, but I was so nervous that Dad was there that I made a huge mistake and got pinned by a guy that I had previously beaten. That hurt me so much, but dad was the best. I'll never forget him saying," That's ok; you will get him the next time". A boy could not have a better father!

    My father spent so much time with me doing everything from fishing to hunting. I went to work with him every time I could. He never once worried about the amount of fish he caught or squirrels he killed because his main concern was that I had a good time. He was the most unselfish person in the world.

    During my senior year I was recruited by some colleges to attend their schools to play football. My family was very different from most of the families in our circle. In my family, there wasn't a question as to whether you would go to college; the only question was where you were going to attend.

My brother went to West Virginia Tech (Tech as the locals called it) and played football there one year. I will never forget going to see him play. The Tech stadium was the biggest I had been in at the time. I was so proud of my brother!

He was the older college guy and came home nearly every weekend. He would pay me a quarter to wash his car or shine his shoes. Believe me, a quarter was a lot of money to me then!

My older sisters went to Christian schools and both married preachers. My mother had a very big impact on our decisions and her opinion was very important to us. Did she expect me to go to a Christian school? My mother made a statement to me that I will never forget. She said that she believed that God had called me to do something. When she said that I thought that the only thing God called anyone for was preaching or singing. I spoke in church many times and sometimes I also sang. She told me that God calls people to do many different things and that I would know His calling for me in His time. Not every Christian is called to preach. It would be many years before I would understand my calling.

It was decided that I would take a football scholarship. I had a few options, but it came down to playing at West Virginia Tech where my brother played. I would receive a full tuition and fees scholarship. In those days, Tech cost around $256 a semester. In 1971, that was lots of money! Compare that to the cost of college today! My scholarship along with

MY THOUSAND MILE JOURNEY

$300 a year from the coal company where my father worked would be some of the money I used for college. I would also work while I was in school.

    Another aspect that I would like to stress about my upbringing is that we were expected to work. We not only worked at home; we would get outside jobs along the way. I remember shoveling snow for neighbors and other odd jobs. The first real job was when I was in junior high school. I worked for the man that was principal at the grade school I attended, Marfrance Grade School. My brother had worked there while in school. The principal and his wife had about 10 acres in Marfrance and our job was cutting grass, washing cars, cleaning house and taking care of the little farm. My brother was paid $.50 an hour and usually worked 40 hours per week. By the time I came along, I got paid $1 an hour and thought that was the most money in the world!

    I also followed my brother in working summers at the local coal company. We worked holidays and weekends, anytime we could to help make ends meet. Before college, much of what I made went to the family. When college started the money went to college expenses.

    I worked at several other places throughout my college career but most of my work was at Gino's Pizza in Montgomery where the college was located. Because of the scholarships and working, I only had to borrow a $150 student loan and paid that back when I graduated.

MY THOUSAND MILE JOURNEY

    In August 1971, I went in early to start football practice, like I did at Greenbrier West. I will never forget that first day and meeting the players I would be competing with for a spot on the team. At Greenbrier West, I was the big guy and didn't have to worry about the competition. Although West Virginia Tech was a small college, it didn't mean that these guys weren't impressive. I have never felt more out of place in my life. How in the world could I compete with these guys, some who were third year starters, for a spot on this team? The other thing was that the first days of practice were in Boomer, WV in nearly 100 F degree weather. After a couple days, we went to three-a-day practices. There were so many days that I wanted to quit and go home. Soon school started and then it became extremely difficult. These classes and football practices were nearly unbearable. I had always played tackle on the football team, but I was a little small for a tackle, so the coach moved me to guard. I made it through summer practice and it was game time. Another thing that was different; I had made it to backup right guard and I knew I would be playing some. The most important thing to me was that I had made the team. That was one of my life's greatest lessons. The fact that if I didn't give up and just kept going, it would be worth it. I will never forget running out onto that field that Saturday in the very stadium and field where my brother had played football. My parents and my brother were there. I couldn't believe that this kid that grew up in little Marfrance, West Virginia could be a college football player! I even lettered that year. The only real problem was that in my first semester my GPA was a 1.67 average. That is not good, and I knew that couldn't continue at that level. The second semester and during spring training I was able to get my grades back up and finished on time. I started most of my career at Tech and worked 40 hours a week. After graduating in four years, I learned that I could accomplish anything I set out to do. As you will see in later chapters, that was really the easiest time of my life. The next chapter will go into detail about real life.

    I make it sound very easy to transition from a very small school to a much larger consolidated school. It was not that simple. Crichton was a more segregated school. We were very used to that and in fact, embraced it. The other schools, however, were not used to it. Having fellow students of different colors was very new to them. Crichton was considered the outside school. I remember that many of the mothers of the other schools at first wouldn't let their daughters date guys from Crichton. In their opinions, we were much wilder. Being an athlete made it a bit easier because we became part of a clique. It was much harder for many of the other students. Making new friends from other schools was much harder.

    In Greenbrier County this change was not as drastic as it was in many other counties in West Virginia or in other states. Having two high schools, the distance students and teachers had to travel was not as drastic. In counties like Pendleton or Pocahontas for example, the travel time was much greater. If a student wanted to be involved in after school programs the travel time would have been extreme. That time and distance makes it hard to connect and stabilize. That's one of the ideals

I really wanted to concentrate on before I move on. In my opinion, connection has become a very real problem in rural America.

One of the themes you will get throughout this entire book is the decline of rural America and the impact that has had on our society. This is a very complex discussion and many factors must be considered. I make no judgments on a whim. I have gone back to before the turn of the previous century. I went to the late 1800s to find out why we have the decline in rural America and related it to my life. Each chapter of this book will deal with this situation.

In order to understand the business model that I am proposing, you must go back many years. Early America consisted of a few large cities and a very large rural footprint. Many small towns were located all over the landscape in every state. Many of them mirrored each other. The main difference was expressed through the immigrant backgrounds of most of the families and people that lived there. Each had a school or several schools of different grade levels. Each had one or more churches. Local stores sold most everything you could need in your daily life. In our case, the coal company owned most of the stores and you used script to buy most of the daily needs like groceries, gas and clothing. The larger items could be bought on time and those funds were taken out of your pay every week.

Most every town had people that focused on certain skills that everyone needed. Some were blacksmiths, woodworkers, clothes-makers, bakers, farmers, etc. Most men had many skills and did much of the work themselves. The actual exchange of money wasn't always the practice. Barter was very important and a common practice. Even many of the doctors, barbers and preachers would take fees out in trade goods. Everyone knew everyone else and knew who they could trust. It was not uncommon to come to the aid of a neighbor in need for many different reasons. I now have over 1,000 friends on Facebook and many of them are the same friends from my childhood who attended the same church and schools.

The real focus of this plan is to provide a mechanism to allow some of the population to be able to move back to these more rural counties. It would allow these people to move back with good jobs and give them the opportunity to make a very positive impact on the local economy and social environment.

CHAPTER 2

SECOND WEEK - FULL SPEED AHEAD

The second week of my journey began on July 22nd and as I did on the first day of my journey, I rode 20 miles. The previous week I felt that I had done quite well by riding 102 miles. Then I started thinking at that pace it would take me ten weeks to complete my journey. Knowing that I had a previous commitment with my sisters on the third week, I figured it would take me until the end of September to finish my journey. That would be okay but I really felt that I could do better.

On that first day of the second week I rode twenty miles from my camp at Renick to Anthony and back. As I was riding down the trail that morning just about three miles from my camp, I saw a beautiful sight beside the trail. One of the best things about the great outdoors is that there are many delicious edibles available to the adventurous. I saw some bright red wild mushrooms growing from an old log beside the trail. These mushrooms are called "Chicken of the Woods" and they are one of my favorites. They are a large meaty type of mushroom and they are very good prepared several ways. I love them coated in beaten eggs, then rolled in flour and fried in olive oil.

During my journey I will share several different wild mushrooms and other fruits and vegetables available to those that will take the time to get out into the great outdoors. Remember that you should take the time to learn what you can eat and what you cannot eat. That is not so easy for many that don't spend much time out in the outdoors or in rural settings. Learn by researching and also by listening. Ask questions and listen to those that know. There are also groups and organizations that are sharing that information online with those that are interested. One of the most important themes of this book is to expand on the importance of eating healthy and organic food. We are entering a great time with the movements to local farming and farm to table eating.

Growing up in rural West Virginia most families had gardens wherever they could grow them. My family didn't have enough land but we searched out little pieces of ground wherever we could, to grow as much as we could. My dad was an excellent gardener and my mother canned everything she could find. I remember building a fire in the back yard with a number three washtub on it and my job was to keep that fire going all day. In that tub were several quart jars of green beans or other veggies that my mother was canning. We didn't have the pressure cooker that most use today. We picked wild strawberries, blackberries, apples, cherries, pears, grapes wild or tame, and any other thing we could put on the table or in a jar. One of the memories that are so entrenched in my mind is the one day in the summer, usually the hottest day, my mother, my grandmother and we kids dressed in long pants and long sleeve shirts. That was the day set aside to pick blackberries. I don't mean a few berries; I mean tubs full of blackberries. I can hardly write about these things because I always fight back tears. Those were precious times! I would love to see my grandchildren do those things and I'm sure they will. Our society would be so much better if children spent time doing these things and a little less time playing video games and surfing social media.

On the next day I rode another 12 miles. I was lucky enough to find another kind of mushroom called "Chanterelles". They are truly perfect mushrooms! This year turned out to be the best summer I ever remember for them. I also found a new mushroom to me that took some time to identify. I always take my time to make sure they are something that I can eat without getting sick or dying. These mushrooms are called "Oyster" mushrooms and they too are delicious.

On July 24th, I rode a part of the trail I had never ridden. Having a camp in Renick, which is located at the 24 1/2-mile marker, we mostly walked or rode the lower part of the trail. I had never ridden above Marlinton and today would be my first time. Believe me; I fell in love with that section of the trail! Beginning at Seebert the trail moves to the east side of the river. The lower 48 miles the trail is on the west side of the Greenbrier River. I drove my car up to Marlinton with my bike in the trunk and parked at the trailhead. The trailhead at Marlinton is located at the 56-mile marker. I started up that stretch and soon found that it would be the most desolate part of the trail. There were large fields and the wildlife was everywhere! At the 62-mile marker I rode up on a majestic black bear as it grazed on fallen apples. I startled it because I was only about 30 feet from it as I approached. The bear jumped up in the air and turned around and ran in the opposite direction. Our state has seen a comeback in the black bear population. During my 1000-mile journey I was able to see 12 black bears and never once did I feel intimidated or afraid. Just past the 65-mile marker, I came upon what is probably the most photographed scene on the trail; the trestle and Sharpe's Tunnel. I had been through the lower tunnel several times but this was the first for this tunnel. The lower tunnel is 402 feet and this one is over 500 feet. The river also moves back to the west side of the Greenbrier. I had to stop and take it all in. I also continued to ride up the trail and at the 67-mile marker I had a flat tire. It was a slow leak and I carried a hand pump so I put some air in it. I turned around and headed back to Marlinton after riding 12 1/2 miles up the trail. As I came back down the trail the tire kept losing air and I would stop and pump it up some more. One of the reasons I picked this bike was that it was very easy to repair. I finally stopped and changed the tube. I always tried to be prepared for any emergency and believe me; you are on your own on that trail. You have no one to call and besides, there is no phone service there! My total ride for that day was 25 miles.

On July 26th, I rode another section of the trail I had never seen. I drove up to Cass with my bike in the trunk. Cass is the northern most trailhead on the Greenbrier River Trail. I had not been to Cass for many years. The last time I was there was to ride the Cass Scenic Railroad up to Bald Knob. (That railroad ride should be on everyone's bucket list!) When I got out of the car and onto my bike, I was so excited! I was able to see the last section of the Greenbrier River Trail where I spent my childhood! It was 42 years since my parents had bought the property at Renick situated next to the rail line that traveled to Cass. That rail line later became the Greenbrier River Trail.

As I followed the trail, the river is narrower than the lower Greenbrier, but it is also crystal clear. I was very impressed with the train station located at Clover Lick. It was empty but in excellent shape.

On this day I traversed the trail south and come upon Sharpe's Tunnel for the second time. The ride south was 17 miles, so my ride was 34 miles on this date. I was getting more and more used to longer rides.

On that Saturday I rode another 31 miles and that brought my total for the second week of my journey to 141 miles. With those 141 miles and the 102 miles on the first week, my grand total now for two weeks was 243 miles. That put me a little over 1/4 of the way to the finish.

I entered the next phase of my life with hopeful enthusiasm. The summer after I graduated from college, I got married. My wife still had three years of school to go before graduation; she was attending the same school that I had attended.

MY THOUSAND MILE JOURNEY

My intention was to become a teacher and coach after college. I loved sports and that seemed to be the next step after playing football in college. I felt it wouldn't be hard to get a job when I graduated, but before I even had time to search for a summer job, I was contacted by a local mining rebuild company and accepted a position to help them start a safety program. Part of my major at Tech was Industrial Safety. This was in 1975 and I was paid $4.00 an hour during that summer. I worked many hours and become very interested in that business. Because of the hours I worked I made pretty good money, especially with all the over-time. I also realized how much or really, how little teachers made in the mid-70s. I was making twice a teacher's salary at the time. Soon I worked my way up to Assistant Shop Foreman and then Foreman.

The first lesson that I learned about work and the chain of command came during college as I worked at a local pizza restaurant. I just made minimum wage and at that time, I think that wage was $1.45 an hour. I also thought the restaurant could not possibly get along without me if I wasn't there. I was the hardest worker there and if I wasn't there it would surely have to close. The assistant manager and I got into a dispute. I knew the manager would side with me, so I quit. I was certain the manager would immediately come get me and hire me back and fire the assistant manager. Well, he didn't do that and I waited for several days and no knock on my door. You know something, that's been 44 years and that restaurant is still open!

Another lesson that I learned after entering the labor force was that I was a very hard worker and a fast learner. I really didn't work that hard in school. I played football, worked and enjoyed a very robust social life. After I began a working career that all changed. I became obsessed with working and advancing my career. I wasn't very interested in money at that time. My wife managed all of our finances and I never really knew how much I made. She was very good at it so I was never bothered with it. I felt that my future was excellent if just kept my nose to the grindstone.

The next lesson came one day when I was working hard. I was the shop foreman and I had no idea how to accomplish that task. I thought that if I worked really hard everyone would see how hard I worked and they would do the same. One day the owner of the company called me up to his office. He had a window in his office that looked down onto the shop floor. He could see everything. I was very dirty and greasy because I was tearing down a shuttle car all by myself. What he told me next changed my life forever. He explained to me that he knew I could outwork anyone there but while I was working myself into an early grave, he wondered what the other people on the floor were doing. Yes, that's right. They were watching me. I explained to him that I would watch him work hard on the floor himself from time to time. He then explained to me that he could do that because he was paying me to make sure the other guys worked. My uniforms after that were much cleaner!

The last lesson was probably the most important lesson I ever learned. The owner of this company and many of the workers were not very educated. The owner only went through the sixth grade and he was one of the smartest people and best fabricators I ever had the privilege of knowing. He could take a tape measurer and build anything. That man and many of the other guys that worked there were experts in many skills. One time I got a call from a company in Cleveland and they wanted a certain frame built for a shuttle car. They were in a hurry so I told them I could be there in a couple days. The gentleman then informed me that he was in Cleveland, England. I didn't have a passport, so I jumped on a plane and headed to Washington, D.C. I called my local congressman and he told me where to go and what to do and I received a passport in one day. The next day I was on a plane headed to England. When I arrived at the mine I went underground and took the needed measurements. After I exited the mine, I called the owner of my company and by the time I got back home he had it built just from my measurements. Most of those guys built their own homes and did all the maintenance on their automobiles. The point of this story is that I learned firsthand that formal education and college was not the only way to learn. The mining industry is one of the most technical industries. College degrees are very important in some areas, especially engineering, but not all employees come from college or universities. The vast majority of the workers come from off the streets and some are offspring of coal miners. Many of them had little formal education but the coal industry did a wonderful job training those men and women to be the best. In mining, profits and production are not the only very important factors; your life depends on you knowing what you are doing.

These experiences and observations are very important to the final conclusions I reach in this book. Late in the 70s I had the opportunity to go to New York City with the president of our company to meet a man that would have a great impact on my life. This man was originally from Hazard, KY and became very wealthy buying radio stations and being highly involved in the entertainment industry. We were asked to come there because he owned some coal property near his home in Kentucky and wanted us to assist him in developing that property. Over the years we became good friends and I made several trips to Manhattan to visit him. That was the first time that I would be introduced to extreme wealth. His office was in the corner of a Times Square Building and he lived in the same building as many stars you would recognize. One of his business partners was the business manager to Muhammad Ali. Needless to say, this country boy was very impressed! The main lesson I learned from all that interaction over the years was that the wealthy and famous are no different than you and me. This man lived in West Palm Beach, FL and worked in Manhattan. Every week he would fly to New York on Monday and on Friday he returned to Florida. I never once wanted to trade my life for his hectic schedule!

 Another thing that I worked on while in the mining industry that helped me with the project I'm working on now was the development of a new type of equipment for underground mining. It may not have been totally new but it was an upgrade from any existing product being used at that time. This was a process that we developed that would turn old shuttle cars into a service vehicle. We also developed a new vehicle from scratch that would help in the servicing of underground equipment. It is very hard, especially in low coal, to carry or drag all of the tools and supplies to each piece of equipment. They must have a dependable schedule for lubrication and scheduled maintenance. This piece of equipment carried all of the lubricants in bulk along with welders, tools, torches, air compressor and other various essentials. The reason that I include this is because this was the first time that I would take a product from inception, through the approval process, through the trial period and then to national sales. The first order we received was a little over one million dollars. It was truly a great experience!

 I don't want to share everything about my time in the coal industry, but it was a very important part of my life and did much to shape who I would become, good or bad. A few years later I started a company that would buy out the original company. We grew fast and my total life was built around work. Little time was spent at home or with my family. That company grew way too big, way too fast! I wasn't ready for that. I made some great achievements but overall I made way too many mistakes. The industry itself was a roller coaster. At certain times money was easy to make and then the coal industry would take a downturn and all of that money and more would be lost.

 By 1987 I couldn't deal with it anymore. It was time to change locations and industries. I moved to Williamsburg, VA because one of my dearest friends lived there. I had nothing and had to start over from scratch. He helped me get a job with a local construction company that put in water and sewer lines. I was a mechanic. After wearing a three-piece suit for several years this was an extremely hard change. The change was not hard prestige wise or hard on my ego, it was hard physically. You see, I was ready for hard work and sweat! I was ready to get very dirty and greasy again and work long hours. The only hard decisions I had to make were what kind of oil to put in a backhoe or other piece of equipment. That work was very good for me. I got back into great physical shape and actually slept at night. I was usually too tired not to sleep. Moving to a different location allowed me to find a new recreational interest. That wasn't very hard in Hampton Roads, VA. Fishing became my passion! Fishing was different there because it was freshwater, but it was also saltwater. I had never salt water fished before but I fell in love with it. Over the last ten years I was too busy working to enjoy my true passions. Never again will that happen!

After working with that construction company for a couple years I got a job with a large paper company. I started at the bottom in an industry of which I knew nothing. The only thing I knew was growing up close enough to Covington, VA was that paper plants smelled horrible! I will never forget the first time I walked into a paper mill. This company had three paper machines. I have always loved large machinery, but these machines were beyond belief! This company employed over 2,000 men and women and made paper from the trees to finished product. I was sent to the area of the mill that recycled the cardboard for reuse. The other thing that I didn't mention was the change in temperature coming from West Virginia to Virginia. It was very hot and humid in that part of the country and I wasn't used to that. Add that to the fact that paper mills are a very hot environment. I got used to it very fast and actually embraced it. This is another manufacturing company that would train most of their people. Making paper is a very complex procedure and the ones that push the buttons must know what they are doing. This was a union company so there was a line of progression that was based on seniority. A person could not move up unless someone died. Very seldom did anyone ever quit. Each person also had to learn other jobs. In a seniority plant if someone was off then the next person in line would be set up to take that position. By learning the next job, a person could make more money.

    I had an opportunity to move to another position after a couple years. A temporary position for a training coordinator came up for bid and I applied for it. In this case, my teaching degree came in handy and I was able to get the position. It was about $5.00 more per hour and it gave me an opportunity to learn at a more rapid pace. This will become very valuable in the business model we will be discussing in greater detail later in this book.

    We will first develop processes to build various products. Then we will write the standard operating procedures and present it in a clear and precise manner. In one of the upcoming chapters, we will spend lots of time on this subject matter. I spent enough time in this department to write the complete training manual that is used today in recycling cardboard fiber into usable paper or cardboard, so I have a lot of experience.

    While at this paper mill, I was able to enroll into a paper making associate degree program. This was a great set of classes that covered multiple areas. Through this work and class atmosphere I developed a love for wood and the various products you can make from it. One of the most important sections that we covered was the making or generating of power. Two things that you must have to make paper are lots of steam and plenty of power. Heat makes steam and steam makes paper. Another cornerstone of this project is the generation of power. We will cover that in great detail in another chapter.

    My time at this paper mill even more beneficial because they offered a Masters of Business Administration (MBA) program. Understand that I was working a union job in a union factory. No matter how much education I attained, that education wouldn't help me move up from a machine to a higher job. The company was going to pay for the whole cost of the two-year program. They were also going to bring the professors to the plant and all of the classes would be on property. Everyone in the program would work for the mill so all the classmates would be familiar (well, there ended up being two from outside.) Out of a thousand union employees, I was the only one that took the company up on their offer. The rest were salaried employees. Remember that I told you when I was in college, I didn't work very hard? I got by barely by the skin of my teeth. This degree program was a totally different story! I worked my tail off and finished with very high marks. This time I wasn't in it for the grades or just to graduate, I was in it to learn. This was a very valuable lesson that we will bring into the new business I am creating.

Learning is a time element. Of great importance are the age and desire of the student and the learning environment. The one thing that made this so interesting to me was the fact that the company offered it to everyone but did not ask for a commitment that you would work for that company for any period of time. It wasn't that I was planning on leaving at the time but I liked the ability to do that.

The MBA curriculum is designed to give the student the ability to one day start and maintain your own business. It also gives you the ability to be a better manager for your employer. This was something that really got my attention! During my time in the mining industry I found that my first love was design and inventing. I could really come up with neat things to invent and build. I said time after time that everyone would want one of these inventions. Wow, I had a lot to learn! If it was that simple everyone would be a millionaire.

I am only in the second chapter and I have totally given away to the whole reason for this book. This is the reason that it's going to take a couple of hundred pages to completely explain what I went through and all the thought processes that brought me to this very business at this very time. If you are patient and thoroughly go through this book, you will get it. It took me several years to develop this concept and I was only able to put it all together during that 1000-mile journey on the Greenbrier River Trail.

While at this paper mill and during this MBA program, I started my first business from scratch. I had run a business and was president of another large business, but this would be my first endeavor from scratch. I will explain in detail how it was put together and the positives and negatives of the startup. Only through success and failure can you reach a higher goal of understanding. Before I go any farther, I want to say that the business I started in 1997 is still viable and will be restarted in time. The lessons I learned and most of the undeniable roadblocks are still there today. The only difference is the times are different. The main reason is that the capitalists of today have made success more possible. There was nothing I could have done to make this product a success then the way I can now. I will explain.

THE PRODUCT

As I told you earlier in this chapter, when I moved to Virginia, I became very interested in fishing again. I grew up loving to fish, especially on the Greenbrier River. Smallmouth bass and trout were my favorite fish. My dad started taking me fishing when I was a small child. I couldn't get enough of it! I would wade in the crystal water. I remember my uncle telling me that I could catch fish in a mud hole. It wasn't until I got out of college and got a real job that I was able to buy a canoe. That was my dream; to be able to put it in the river and float down like the wealthier kids would do. I wore that aluminum canoe out! I used it in lakes, ponds and rivers. When I moved to Virginia things changed somewhat. Of course, I took my old aluminum canoe. There were several differences. One was that I was older and a little heavier now. That canoe that used to be very stable was not as stable. The water was bigger here and had moving tides. I fished a lot in the winter. Many times I would break the thin sheets of ice to fish. I lived on a canal that had the best largemouth bass fishing water I had ever seen, especially in the winter. It seemed that the larger bass would come up in that canal then because the water was warmer there than in the James River.

I would watch the big bass boats coming up in that canal and those guys and ladies would stand on the front or rear of that boat and seem so comfortable. I also knew that these boats cost many thousands of dollars. It wasn't that I would never be able to afford one; I just didn't think I would ever spend that much money on a bass boat. One reason was because I never saw one of those people catch close to the amount or size of the big fish I caught!

So, being the inventor that I was, I started thinking. How could I turn this little canoe into a small bass boat? How could I make this little canoe stable enough for me to stand and not turn over? This was the time for research. That's what I do when I start to design. First, I have to know what's out there. If someone already makes it I would just buy it and not waste my time building it. These items would be called pontoons in most stores. I could not find anything that I really liked so I started researching history. I saw what the Hawaiians and Polynesians used and wondered why they only had the pontoons on one side. I found that the main reason was that their center of gravity was toward that side and it wasn't important for them to turn fast. They basically went in one direction. The other reason is that the weight of that pontoon would help hold the craft upright.

Now I finally figured that there was not a product that would completely fit my desires or needs. Most people invent things that they want or need. (This is the process that I have gone through on several products that we will be manufacturing in this business.) The first thing that I did was buy a couple of inflatable boat buoys that people put on the side of their boats to protect them from other boats or docks. I made a metal rack that went across my canoe in the middle and fastened the buoys to each end. This kind of worked because I might not turn over by leaning but definitely couldn't stand up. I had two choices with these pontoons. I could position them in the water so that the boat wouldn't rock so much and I could probably stand up depending on the size of the pontoons. The problem with that was that when I tried to paddle through the water they would really hold me back. The great thing about a canoe is that it takes very little effort to paddle it through the water. The other option was to fasten them higher up but again the canoe would be very rocky when I was trying to fish.

Then it hit me as great ideas tend to do if you think about them enough. My pontoons had to be movable! They had to elevate to whatever I was doing at the time. They needed to be up when I was moving and down when I was fishing. That sounds simple enough. With enough time and money, I was able to figure it out. I perfected the design and was able to obtain a patent on this product. I changed the name from pontoons to stabilizers. This was all accomplished while I was working at the mill and still in the MBA program.

The first and most critical decision that I had to make is whether these stabilizers would be marketed as an add-on or as a full bass boat. I decided to market this as a full bass boat made from a canoe hull. I started out by making a very big mistake. I turned down the easier product and the one that could hit the market very fast for one that would cost so much money and take a very long time to produce. (You will see in this business most of the research has been completed and test products have been made.) Making the whole boats was a great Idea and we built some great boats. We also later made the stabilizer kits that we eventually sold around the world through our own website and through Cabala's. This new business will again make and market both of these products because all the mistakes have already been made and we now know our market and customer base.

The part of this business that I really want to discuss is the market area of the whole boats. This is one of the main reasons that I came up with this business model. The boats were beautiful and many folks wanted them. We marketed them through the Outdoor Channel with a local Virginia Beach fishing show. Whenever this show would air we could not answer the phone fast enough. Hundreds of people would call with their credit card in hand. The problem was that these calls came from all over the United States and Europe. There would be two calls from Alaska, two or three from Arizona and four from Boston area. The distance between this customer bases was insurmountable. I tried so hard to set up a dealer network. That is the way most boats are sold. It usually costs the manufacturer at least 30% of the total market price to sell through a distributor. That is not the only consideration that the manufacturer has when it comes to picking or even finding a distributor. The other question is obstacle is that the manufacturer needs to find a distributor. In our case with these boats, they were only sold to a smaller market than most other boats. First, they were sold mostly to those that liked fishing in small boats and second, it was mostly sold to those that paddled or used trolling motors.

    This is one of the main concepts that we are dealing with when I had the idea of this new business. With the advent of the Internet, direct sales to the consumer became much more available to small manufacturers. Anything that could be shipped by traditional carriers like USPS, FedEx or UPS allowed a manufacturer to sell in quantities of one or more. The problem we had with the boats and with many of our products that we will be making in the future is that these are large products including boats, furniture and even houses. This whole concept is a hindrance to most small manufacturers or mom and pop startups. How do you get the product in an assembled state without requiring the customer to spend time putting it together? In another chapter, we really spend time with this situation. What is normally a true road block is becoming a real plus for this business!

So far in this chapter, we have covered two of my careers. Most people have only one career during their lifetime and a few have two. In my case I had four completely different careers that each spanned several years. After completing my 9th year with the paper mill and the boat business, the paper mill that I worked for sold out to a Canadian company. I lost the permanent position that had taken up 8 of those 9 years. So instead of starting at the bottom again, I decided to take a chance and leave the mill and work full time in the boat business. That was an extremely hard decision and one that kept me awake for many hours. That's when I got my first experience with raising capital for a startup. As president of the mining equipment company, I handled millions of dollars and worked with some of the largest banks in the country. This was a whole different world. There is one lesson that you must learn very quickly when starting a new business. There are only two ways to raise capital for a new business: debt or equity. You must either borrow money or sell equity in your business. Both of those are very hard to do. You are not established, so banks will not even talk to you. If they do, the interest they will charge makes it impossible to make money. As this chapter is mostly about my experiences and the opportunities I had to deal with most of the many facets of business, I can say that I have done it all. Some of the ways I raised capital worked. Some were the right thing to do and some were not. I'm not going to spend more time in this chapter about raising funds because that is in an upcoming chapter. One of the aspects of this business that I spent the most time on was how we were going to raise the startup money and raise enough funds to keep the company going through the predictable lean years until we can establish a nest egg or war chest.

    Starting and running that company was an amazing experience! We had many ups and downs that included our own television show and our own magazine. We also had two outdoor retail stores and an Internet sales company. I always thought bigger is better. The problem is that I pushed things faster than the available capital. Don't worry about it because sales will make up the difference!

    Living on the edge seemed to me my motto. That was fine until September 11, 2001 and everything changed for everyone! Granted, we were already operating on the edge. Some weeks we were not making payroll on time and were behind on accounts payable. Then, overnight you lose almost all your advertising sales and your main investor runs into problems of his own. Our company operations were in Somerset, PA. We were just a few miles from where Flight 93 went down. That day influenced every person in America and many around the world. I will never forget that day for the rest of my life! I had to travel to Johnstown, PA that morning to a meeting. As I got into the car, the radio sounded an alert that one of the World Trade Center towers had been struck by a plane. Just a few miles up the road an alert announced that the second tower was also hit by a plane. Hearing this, a feeling of fear and uncertainty spread all over me. Before we would reach our destination, another alert came on the radio. A third plane had flown into the Pentagon. We just had about 30 miles to travel so we continued driving until we reached our destination in Johnstown. Cell phones weren't working and just as we entered the office the alert came over the radio. With fear in his voice, the announcer told us that a plane had crashed near Somerset, PA. It actually went down in Shanksville about two miles from where I lived. This was a very drastic occurrence and a feeling that I will never completely lose. America was completely changed in just a few hours. In just a short period of time our nation became afraid of everything and everybody.

    We were able to keep this project going for a couple more years, but we closed operations in early 2003. This did not end my work on that project because I had made stabilizers available to the general public. Sales were still going through Cabala's and through the Internet. I soon sold the rights to a company in Pennsylvania and received a commission for some time before they went out of business. I moved back to West Virginia and then later back to Williamsburg, VA. (More details are to follow in the next chapter.)

In keeping with the boat career, I went to work for Tracker Boat Company. Tracker Boats is owned by Bass Pro Shops and I was able to obtain that job because I got to know the manager of the Hampton, Virginia store while being a vendor at several boat shows in the area. He was familiar with my products and my sales ability. I had never sold a boat except the ones that I had built and really had lots to learn. I really didn't know much about bigger boats and Tracker was the largest manufacturer of boats. They had bass boats, pontoon boats, ski boats, and salt water boats. They also sold Artic Cat 4-wheelers. Every time I start something new, I start studying that business. I spent some time studying boats in general and then I started studying Tracker Boats. I studied the competitors and our strengths and weaknesses. I really wanted to be able to do a very good job at this. Something new to me was that I was very nervous! I'll never forget my first customers as a Tracker salesman. I was in my nice white shirt with Tracker and all of the other patches from the other boat company on it. I looked like a billboard and was so proud. I had met the owner of the company a few years earlier and he was someone that I admired. He had started that company from scratch in Springfield, Missouri and Bass Pro and Tracker Marine was a model of excellence!

    I was paid a small salary and 2% commission on all my sales. I had never been paid a commission before, so that was new to me. I knew a $200 weekly salary was quite low and I couldn't make it on that alone and was not really sure how I would do selling these boats. I did very well from the very start. I figured out a system and I stuck with it the whole time was there. I learned something as a young man and it guided me very well through life. It was a saying that I heard that really stayed in my mind. This saying was by a famous Supreme Court Justice and to paraphrase he said, "I wouldn't give a fig for simplicity on this side of complexity, but I would give my life for simplicity on the other side of complexity." Think about that for a few minutes. When you start something, and it seems so hard, you can look back at it once you master it and say to yourself; Wow, that was a piece of cake! I felt that way the first time I went scuba diving. I was scared to death! I didn't think I could ever learn something so hard, but I conquered my fear and you can too! You just need to be positive from the beginning!

    The way Tracker works in their boat sales is that it is one price for everyone. No matter whom you know and regardless of how much money you have in the bank you get the same price. Paying cash is something they don't like because they make money on financing. Once I learned that concept it made my job much easier. I also realized very quickly that most people that come into a Bass Pro Shop are not there to buy a boat and if they do, they are first-time boat buyers. They would come in with a printout off the Internet of the boat they wanted and the cost. They usually had in their minds which boat they wanted down to exact color. These were my two main obstacles. The first situation that I had to learn to deal with was the price. Although I said the price was set, it was usually advertised with a small motor. That pre-pricing made the boat look very inexpensive but that motor was not the best choice for that boat. I quickly learned how to explain that. The second situation that I had to learn to deal with was the fact that that boat they had their heart set on was probably not in stock at this particular store. Each store had their inventory sent earlier in the year and that inventory was pre-determined. It took a long time to order an out of stock boat and have it delivered to the store. So, I had two choices and the first was to see if I could change their minds on the boat style and color to another boat that we did have in our inventory. Any salesperson could do that but the second thing I would do set me apart from most of the other salespeople. If there was a boat that matched the style they had in mind at another Tracker location I would have it transferred to our location or pick it up myself. I was on the road a lot of the time. Remember, I was on commission and they furnished the truck and the gas to go get the other boat.

  I was a top-five salesperson in the world for Tracker every year I was there. I really think the main reason wasn't that I was that much a better salesperson; it was that I worked harder. Most of the other salespeople didn't like working nights or weekends. I quickly learned that was when I could sell the most boats. That was the time that most husbands and wives could come in together and view these expensive boats. In most cases, that was a family decision and it was perfect to have both spouses there at the same time.

  Another thing I learned very quickly was that these potential buyers were not just first-time buyers; they probably didn't know very much about operating a boat. These were speed boats and most of the waters around Hampton Roads were brackish water. That's the water line dividing salt and fresh water. It was tidal water and that means that the water level would change drastically several times each day. The difference between low and high tides could be several feet. That means the places you could drive your boat now may not be high enough to drive it in a few hours. Most of these potential buyers had no idea how to drive a boat trailer and how to take the boat off and put it back on the trailer. These, too, were lessons that I had to learn as part of my sales regiment. I questioned every customer very hard from the beginning to learn their knowledge and experience in these areas. If they wanted to buy a boat from me, I promised them that I would help them learn these things. When they came to the store to pick up their boat one of Tracker's specialists would completely take them through their boat and explain everything about it. That would usually take about an hour and then they would call me. Even if it was my day off I would come in and I would take the new owners about five miles down the road to a boat ramp on the James River or if I was delivering the boat to them we would go to their local boat ramp. We would put the boat in the water. I would make them go through everything. I would just show them the ropes and help them with their confidence. We would then get in the boat and I would let them start it up. We would go for a really good ride as I explained what each buoy meant and on which side you were to take your boat. At that time, if I felt comfortable with their ability, I would have them take me back to the dock and I would let them go out by themselves. I would wait there or go back to the shop if it we were close. I would give them my cell phone number and they were to call me when they finished so I could meet them back at the dock. The reason I would meet them back at the dock was that they usually needed help with loading the boat back onto the trailer. We would do that several times until we all felt comfortable. On several occasions, I would meet them again to go over it yet again. In four years at Tracker, I never had one unsatisfied customer! The way going the extra mile helped me sell more boats was that these folks would go out and tell their friends. I remember on many Saturdays or Sundays there would be maybe five or more families waiting on me to sell them a boat.

God gave me the ability to communicate with other people and if you know me, you know that I have never met a stranger! One of the traits that I learned and developed over the years will be taught to all of our salespeople in this new company. That is one thing I promise!

This was a great job and I made good money, but it was time to change once more. I left the last career because the company sold out and I lost my permanent job. The reason I left this career was another thing out of my control. As I previously stated, I worked mostly on commission. One day as I walked into work I was informed by the boat manager that Tracker Marine was changing the way they paid their salespeople. Instead of salary plus commission, Tracker would be going to an hourly pay for all salespeople. So I went from over a $100,000 a year to $10 an hour. All I will say is that it was a great move for Tracker!

As with the last change in careers I accepted it and moved on. Change is not something that I feared. With all three of my career changes, I now see that it was all in God's plan. My dad was alone now because my mother had passed away in 2003 and he was quite lonely. My second marriage had failed and I was alone. It was time to move back to West Virginia. I haven't spent time in this book talking about my marriages and it will not happen. That's not the purpose of this book. I will say that I take full responsibility for both failures. I really embraced moving back to my home state. I loved being closer to my wonderful father. His health was still good, so I didn't move in with him. I decided to live at our camp in Renick and he continued to live in Rainelle. We talked every day and most days I would go over there or he would come to the camp. I made many trips over there late in the evening because he tended to accidentally leave the phone off the hook and I couldn't stand not knowing if he was all right or not. He also had trouble with his remote, so I would get a call and I would run over and fix it. I really loved doing things for him. There will be much more about him in the next chapter.

That is still my passion and I really believe that after all these years I have the solution. I'm not going to go too deep into this career at this time. In chapters 3, 4, and 5 we will be looking at this career in great detail because that is the present and last one. The building of these houses and all the other products that I have mentioned are the main focus of this business plan that I am detailing in this book.

CHAPTER 3

THIRD WEEK - TIME TO RE-GROUP

The first two chapters of this of this book are about my history. The first chapter dealt with my early years and the major factors and experiences that directed my childhood development. It started at my birth and continued throughout my undergraduate years. The second chapter was about my work history and the many careers that I had throughout my life. The reason that it is important for you to understand the many life changes that I went through is to help you to understand how the decision-making processes brought me to the current and future businesses that I am starting.

The third chapter is also about history and how my life changed and continues to change to this day. I believe God directed me to this place in my life that is now centered on doing His will. I also believe that each of those decisions helped bring this together in the last few months. This very important 1000-mile journey was the cornerstone of this process. All these years and all this information was tangled in a mind that was struggling on making the next move. If I had to put a label on my life up to a few months ago I would have to say that I was a failure in many ways. I have been called a genius, a crook, a con man and a great mind. At times I could explain things with the certainty of the greats of our times and yet, things never totally came out the way I explained it. This chapter is about the way I stopped and re-grouped. The focus is on how I changed my life and my thought process to really be in the center of God's will and do something that would be of great service to the people of this world. Most of all I want it to be to the glory of God and His ministry.

    The rest of this book will be about the future and how everything fits into place so that this too won't be a failure. This could become one of the largest companies in the world and that can only be accomplished with the guidance of God and being able to bring in the right people to help. This book is written not only to raise capital and to sell its products, but to get people excited about getting involved in the startup! There are great minds out there that have the same compassion as I do about the future and many of them are wandering through life just like I did and searching for something to fill a void. There are retired people that still have energy and tons of experience that they want to share with the newer generations. As a society we have put them out to pasture way too early and we need to get from them whatever we can to help us continue. No one will ever be considered too old to join our team and we will respect the time they have already given to us. This company will be involved in nearly every aspect of the business community from manufacturing, banking, health, education, accounting, engineering, agriculture, forestry, power generation, construction, social working and much more! This will all be explained in the next few chapters.

    The third week of my thousand-mile journey started on July 29th and this week had been set aside several weeks earlier to be a reunion of sorts for my three sisters and myself to get away and spend some time together. My youngest sister had a time share that she could use, and she picked a beautiful resort in upstate Pennsylvania for us to meet. I was really looking forward to it and later in this chapter I will fully explain why it was so important for us to share this time.

    I didn't need to leave for our get together until Monday morning, so I had the itch to get on my bike and ride. I will be talking all through this book of how important it is to get as much physical activity as possible. This is just my 15th day of this journey and it is already becoming a very important part of my life. I couldn't wait to get out there and ride as hard and long as I could go. I used to tell my dear brother, that passed away way too young, that he should get off the chair and walk. He was an accountant by trade that required sitting at a desk for hours at time. During tax season he would sit for days and do one tax return after another without leaving his chair. I would tell him to walk 50 feet today and then try 51 tomorrow. There is never a day that goes by that I don't miss him very much! So, you see how you take care of your body and your health affects many people other than yourself. I picked this first day of the third week to ride my farthest. I got up early and really didn't have a plan of how far I wanted to ride so I headed up the trail and rode to the 34-mile marker. It was a beautiful day and I felt so good! I turned around there and rode back to my camp. That totaled 20 miles. I had a little lunch and drank plenty of water and decided I wasn't even close to finished for the day, so I then decided to head down the trail and see how far I could go. One thing about riding the trail is that when you go from a certain place like my camp, you still had to go back. I rode to Anthony which was located at the 14 ½ mile marker and that made a total of 40 miles for the day. That was a good ride and although I would be gone most of the week, I had a good number to add to my total and 40 miles closer to the 1,000 miles.

The next day, I traveled to Pennsylvania to meet with my sisters. During that week I worked out at the gym everyday so I wouldn't lose any of the conditioning I had obtained. My sisters and I had a wonderful time and I got in some great gym time. I'm not going to write about the time I spent with my sisters but in those few days we bonded stronger than ever and that closeness will endure forever.

As I explained at the beginning of this chapter this was a week that I wouldn't get a lot of riding in towards my goal. There are interruptions to our plans from time to time and we must take breaks in our lives to re-group. In early 2004, not too long after 9/11 my business was failing, and I didn't know what to do next. It was only a few months after the loss of my dear mother. I knew I needed to change my life and just moving to a different location and a finding new job wouldn't fix it. I was so unhappy with my life at that time. I was letting down some great friends because I couldn't focus on anything but getting my life back together. I was working on some big business deals, but everything seemed to go in the wrong direction. It is so hard to make promises you know you probably can't keep. That is so easy to do in business because those things that you hope for and dream about don't always work out no matter how hard you try. It was time for something drastic to happen! No, suicide was never on my mind. I did something that I had done before, I started walking. I was driving a very close friend's vehicle and I just left it in a parking lot in Cumberland, MD and didn't tell anyone where I was or where I was going. I thank God that she is still my very close friend. I don't deserve it. Another person in that town I let down forgave me and I thank God every day for that too. I just needed to be completely alone and try to figure some things out. I started praying and walking. This was not the first time I did that and not the last time. I had no money in my pocket, no spare clothes, no food and just a destination in mind. I had nearly 200 miles to go because the camp on the Greenbrier River was my destination.

There's a movie that my dad and I loved about Sargent York. Sargent York was the most decorated soldier in WWI. When he was confronted with a very hard decision to make, he and his old hound dog would go up on this mountain for as many days as it took for him to figure out things. He wanted to learn what God's plan was for him and how he was to proceed with his life. Well I didn't have a hound dog, so it was just me and God. God's plan is not something that has a roadmap or an instruction booklet. Even if you figure it out it is not always easy to stay on that course. One undeniable fact is that if you are working for God and you get out of that plan, He will let you know. I did that again a few years later.

I started walking as long and as far as I could that day. I walked and cried the whole way. As darkness fell, I was so tired that I just walked over into a ball field and into the dugout and lay on the bench and fell asleep. I had probably walked about 30 miles and it was so hot that day. It seems funny that as hot as it was that some days it was just as cold at night. I woke up in the night so very cold! I made it until daylight and I started walking again. I never really got hungry, but my feet were starting to hurt. I never actually put out my thumb and hitchhiked like I did in my early years, but a young man picked me up that afternoon and I rode with him about 25 miles to where he worked. Then I got out and started walking again. I walked again until dark and I had just got into the area where my youngest sister once lived and this time I went into the woods. I did find an old long-sleeved shirt that someone had thrown out on the side of the road. It was a heavy wool shirt that was quite warm, and I picked it up and started carrying it with me. It was dirty, but I knew I would need it that night. I went into the woods and found a great place to lie down but first I got on my knees and started praying. When you get really low and you know you have let down many people and especially God, it becomes very hard to ask God for forgiveness and for His help fixing things. It's not hard for God; it's hard for man because God is so forgiving and is always there for us. Pride is the first thing that you must shed to get back into God's will. Being hungry, wearing dirty clothes and shoes that are about to fall off your feet will help you do that. That wool shirt might have been a little dirty but I'm telling you it really felt good that night!

    The next day was day three of my journey and the next morning two ladies stopped and asked me if I wanted a ride. I happily got into their car. They drove me another 15 miles and I got out and started walking again. I was now in Pocahontas County, so I knew I was getting closer to my destination. No one knew where I was and where I was going and that was the way I wanted it. My Dad lived in Rainelle and I knew the camp would be empty unless he just happened to go over there to cut the grass or something. We had just lost my Mom the September before and my Dad was still mourning so much. I didn't really want to put another burden on him, so I hoped that he wouldn't be there. It seemed like I was always a burden on my family. I was always so unsettled and always searching for something. I'll never forget the next few hours walking along the Jackson River. It was such a long day. It seemed like I walked an hour or so between the occasional motorists. I didn't actually want a ride, but it seemed so lonely. I was still very distraught and very depressed as I walked beside the road that day. I was really getting to the point of exhaustion and was very dehydrated. I had not had anything to eat in three days and very little to drink but I just kept walking. I would chew on grass blades to help put some moisture in my mouth as I walked. I remember eating the top buds off the milkweed plants along the road because they are very tasty. I know there were many things that I could have eaten but that really wasn't on my mind. I was just wondering how I could have made so many mistakes and how I could change the way I did things going forward. That night I camped in the woods again, but this time I did take the time to build a fire. That was a good thing because this night it was very cold, and it rained off and on the entire night.

The morning of the fourth day I decided I would really try to get to the camp. I walked about ten miles and then I got a ride down to Route 92 below Green Bank. From there I walked a couple more miles and for the first time I put my thumb out. A very nice, interesting man and his wife picked me up and they happened to be going to the Veterinarian that is not far from Frankfort. We had a nice conversation and they gave me lots of encouragement. It seems like God always sends the right people your way when you need them the most. With the help of one more ride, I found myself at my destination. I was never so happy to see that small building we called our camp! There was not very much to eat there but I did have some crackers with mustard on them. That doesn't sound too delectable but when you haven't eaten in four days you will eat anything! I waited a couple days until I had the nerve to call Dad and tell him I was at the camp. He came over and was so helpful to me without giving me a hard time.

The camp was the best place for me to spend time and really get my head on straight. I had friends there that were truly good friends. I picked up a part-time job with a local friend that had lots of land and many cattle. I helped build fences and whatever needed to be done. That's when I first realized that riding a bike on the Greenbrier River Trail was very healing. I rode many miles on the days I wasn't working and got back into very good shape physically and was still working on my head. My brother came by and we talked, and my sisters also came up and really helped me out. I could never believe that I came from the same mom and dad as they did because I was so different. They were so settled and disciplined in their lives and their families and then there was me.

    My youngest sister and the rest of the family decided that I needed to go back to Williamsburg, VA and live with her for a while until I got settled in what I wanted to do next. I continued my bike riding down there and really got into it. I soon found one job and then the opportunity to join Tracker Boats came up and I jumped on it and that part of the re-group was over.

    I had changed through all that time period and became closer to God and wanted to find out what God had in store for me. It would still take me several years before that became apparent to me. I was now working and making pretty good money and you would think that happiness was there for me to grasp but it still wasn't that easy. When my second marriage failed, I made a decision that I would never get into another relationship. One of the things that haunted me for many years was the breakup of my first marriage. I'm not going to get into any details about that marriage or the breakup, but I will tell you that I left that relationship leaving two beautiful little girls.

To this day I still regret that decision. I had a great relationship with my second wife and she had five beautiful girls which I love to this day and always will. It just seems like my life has always been such a failure. I made the decision that whatever time I had left in this world I would always be there for my daughters and my step-daughters. There was no need to bring anyone else into my heart and life. I thank God every day that all of them are doing quite well and I could not be prouder. That decision was the right decision, but it left me very lonely from then on.

As you are probably starting to understand I am a unique individual. I am a very deep person and my mind never shuts down. I am more like my mother than anyone I know. My mother was a deep person and very well read. She was an intelligent person that finally let her thoughts and fears get the best of her. I could hear praying into the night concerning things that would never worry most of us. She was a deeply spiritual person and with some help later was able to control those fears.

This Chapter is about a re-grouping but more important it is about a transformation or maybe a preparation; a period that I believe God was preparing me for something beyond what I could have possibly accomplished without Him. During the time I spent at the camp after I left Pennsylvania, I started having these dreams. I still have them today and they are quite vivid. I can go into this state of mind even in the daytime when my mind is totally immersed in thought. At night when I start having this dream, it becomes so real that I wake up in the middle of the night and continue with this dream or line of thought for hours. At first, I had great fear of this dream and then after a few years I began to look forward to it. Normally a dream that lasts this long is very tiring, but this dream has become my greatest friend. I look forward to every part of it. This dream is like a business plan of sorts; it started out very slowly and moved forward in a very precise manner as to a continuation or a call to action. This plan, as you will see if you really study this book, is beyond my small mind. I believe, beyond any shadow of doubt that God himself is behind this plan.

THE DREAM

The dream started out of the blue one night. In the dream, I found myself living in a very small town, not unlike the small town where I spent my childhood. The only real difference was that instead of living on a hill, I lived in a beautiful valley. It was a wonderful little town with schools, churches, stores and city government buildings. It was the perfect little town with great friends and good neighbors. A small river ran through it like the river that runs beside our camp. At the upper end of this little town there was a dam that held back this river and made a very large lake. The lake was a very big financial windfall for the community and much of our lives were surrounded by activities involving the lake. There was a beautiful trail that traversed along the side of the river to the bottom of the dam and I used to walk on it all the time. I used to fish at the bottom of the dam and spent many hours there by myself.

This is the picture I have always had in my mind every time the dream comes to me. The background never changes and the dam itself is always the same. In the very first dream, this was the picture and it was very vivid. It seemed like I had made several trips to the bottom of the dam but on this certain trip I noticed something very different about the dam. There was a small crack in the dam wall. This crack went up several feet from the bottom and it was quite high over my head. It was very hard to notice. That was as far as it went in that dream. The next day, and for several consecutive days thereafter, I could not get that whole picture out of my mind. I could see it so clearly. I could see the people, but they were not the people of my town. It seemed like I lived in a completely different town than the one where I grew up. As I relate this very long and complicated dream to you, I will try to give you the interpretation that I get from each part. I always believed that this was the world in general. It didn't depict a specific town.

The next time I had this dream was quite a while after the first one. The dream started as I was in town and I was going to walk back up to the dam bottom again. As I walked, I was picturing in my mind the small crack that I saw in the dam wall. As I got closer it started to come into sight and I was totally focusing on that exact spot where I remembered the crack to be. When I got closer, I could see that the crack was a little larger. It wasn't much larger but the main difference this time was that there was just a little more water leaking through the crack that wasn't there the first time. This made the crack much more real.

In this dream, I didn't do anything about seeing this crack expansion as the dream again ended but I could not get this out of my mind. Weeks passed before the next dream. You need to understand that this dream or series of dreams has been going on for about 15 years. The majority of this business plan has come to me at night in dreams or during many sleepless hours with this plan totally engulfing my mind.

The next dream would enter a whole new phase of this process. As I made the next trip to the bottom of the dam, I was truly amazed at how much the crack had grown and how more water was seeping through the crack. I knew I then had to do something, but I wasn't sure how to proceed. I went back to the town and started telling some of my neighbors. There was one thing that I didn't mention about this dream. I never had a family or a place that I lived in this dream. I believe the dream was always supposed to be generic and the lessons that would come from it were more general. As a matter a fact there was never anyone in this dream that I personally knew. I believe that is why to this day I don't talk about politics or any particular politician in any of my writings. This dream and this complete business plan has been in the developmental stage through so many different administrations that I would have to change it too many times. This book and this plan are about the people and what we need to do to bring about change. I mean that this is about a new beginning that doesn't necessarily mean that everything is wrong. Even in this series of dreams it was about "seeing is believing and believing is seeing". (Yes, I heard that in a movie but I don't remember which one!)

When I told my friends and neighbors, they didn't take me very seriously. As a matter a fact, I couldn't even get them to go look with me. They would say that the dam had been there for many years and would still be there when we are dead and gone. I was looked at like the kid that cried wolf and I was hurt. I will never forget that when this dream ended my whole thought process changed. I began to have a more practical approach to this dream. The first couple of times I dreamed that I could see it and no one else would even look at it really made me self-conscious. I just kept thinking that it was about me and the fact that I often came up with ideas and no one took me seriously. That was something that I lived with in real life. Was this dream meant to tell me that I see things that aren't really there and that I should just keep those things to myself or did it have a different meaning? I tried to put it out of my mind and move on. I thought that if I quit thinking about it, I would quit having this dream. Well, of course, that didn't work and as a matter of fact, it wasn't long before another dream came to me. This time I found a few people that would finally go with me to the bottom of the dam. This was the most amazing dream because I will never forget that moment when we reached the exact spot where I first noticed the crack. As we stood there, I said nothing. The silence was deafening as I was patiently waiting for a positive response. I just knew they were going to say they saw it and ask what they could do to help fix it. The exact opposite happened as each one of them had the same response. They didn't see anything different from the rest of the dam wall. As I stood there speechless, I was totally at a loss for words. I could see it as clear as I could see them standing there. I questioned them several times and even walked closer to the spot and kept pointing to the exact spot that was so vivid and clear to me. How could they not see something so unmistakably present? I remember as we walked away, I looked back over my shoulder and got a last glimpse to reassure myself that what I believed was there, was in fact, there.

In the next days after this dream I tried so hard to find the meaning of what I had seen in this dream. I was way beyond believing that this was really about a dam and I knew beyond the shadow of a doubt that God had a message and I needed to figure it out. The first thought was that the vision that I was having was about salvation itself and that becoming a Christian is something so clear that everyone should easily see it too. (More about this thought later.)

The next dream continued as I was going through town telling as many people as I could about what I had seen. I remember how vivid and real the conversations were with these people. What was unusual about this series of dreams was again the fact that there were folks that I didn't know. Normally dreams seem to be about people that you know or to whom you can relate. How does your mind come up with new people that you seem to know? Each day I would go back to my spot and look at the dam. The crack got bigger and bigger and more water was flowing through it. I would get other people to go with me and they could not see anything. I remember that it got so bad that I decided to move to a higher location. There was no doubt in my mind that if that dam would break all below would lose their lives. I remember how afraid I was to go into the town because I thought it could break at any time and I could not get out fast enough. I finally arranged a meeting with the town council and explained my fears to them and again that fell on deaf ears. This dream process went on for some time and it seemed like it was very important for me to continue to think of what I could do to change the minds or the view of the people so I kept trying.

It was sometime later when the dreams changed. I remember it so vividly; the first time that someone else saw what I saw. It was so unusual how it happened. This person didn't go up with me. He had heard about my experience and in fact someone told him, laughing, that I actually believed that there was a crack in the dam. The difference in this case was that this person had actually seen it on his own and was afraid or unwilling to tell anyone. When he heard that I was the person who saw the crack he came to me. I admit that for the first time I felt validated and refreshed. More and more people came to us and related stories of how they, too, saw the crack. One night I had a dream that the town council called me in. They said, "Okay, we now believe that there is a crack in the dam wall, but we believe that it is not serious, and nothing needs to be done about it." They seem to have brought in some experts and each one of them gave opinions that matched their beliefs. They said, "It's there, but don't worry about it because it would take years for it to get serious. Let someone else deal with it later."

    Earlier I was writing about the meaning of these dreams and how my life was impacted through them. I stated that my first thought was that these dreams were about salvation and of course, the logical answer was that I should become a preacher or an evangelist. I should share with the world that salvation is real and that God is coming back and we need to be ready. Although I believe that with all my heart, I never did feel that was my calling. I even went through a time when I spoke in many churches and I sang all the time in church. I loved it and I offered myself to full time work in the church. It consumed my thoughts and I could draw a crowd with my enthusiasm. My mom always warned me that I could get too into church and it could become all about me and not the message. She told me time and time again that not everyone that is called by God is called to preach or sing. I really struggled with that throughout my life. If God called me into business or as an inventor, why was I having so many problems and why wasn't I more successful? By the time you finish with this book, I hope I have explained it so that you understand. God's plan is not always instant, and it doesn't always provide immediate gratification.

    The dream changed in the months and years after Hurricane Katrina. This part is very hard for me to explain in detail. The dream itself never changed from the crack in the dam and the seriousness of it but the interpretation I got from it did change. (Water plays a big part throughout this book.) As I talked to the folks that were from the Lower 9th Ward in New Orleans, my heart was filled with their pain. I started studying the effects of hurricanes, tornadoes and floods in general. These dreams and this thought process have continued uninterrupted since that tragedy. It has expanded to include so many other areas and does include the effect it can have on many others. My main focus has become more about how this tragedy affects the poor, the lower middle class and the middle class itself. It does affect the upper class, but they have many more resources to deal with these tragedies than do the other classes of people. It is not that I want to disregard the upper class; it's just that I don't believe God has led me to focus on them. They could, however, benefit greatly from the things we are proposing.

    The next series of dreams became about how we could get the message out that there was a problem that needed to be fixed. It is so much like the housing industry. We have not really improved the way we build houses in the past decades to account for the effects of these storms. They have addressed the problem somewhat but still need to go much further. Our conclusions on this matter will be thoroughly detailed in the next chapter. It is like the dam in my dreams. Some think there is a problem but it is not something we can address at this time. It is also believed that it would cost way too much money to address. Some believed that we were saying that the only answer was to start over and completely build a new dam.

That is not at all what we were saying. We were just looking for a dialog. The other thing that really came out in the dream was that there were people that would come forward and have good ideas and seemed to really want to get involved in the process; however, once you started to depend on them, they would disappear. I have seen that many times while working on this project.

I remember that there was a series of dreams in which I went to the rich people that lived on the hill above the dam. They knew there was a problem and they had some sympathy, but it didn't really affect them as much. I went to other parts of the state and they didn't want to get too involved in our problem either.

This is the part of the dream where I really want to make a point. I started dreaming about finding a solution to the situation within those of us who were really affected and the ones that could benefit from a solution. In the dream, those of us who saw the crack really wanted to fix it, so we started having regular meetings to discuss a solution. These dreams were exhausting because they seemed to take all night. They were really a discussion where I talked and listened. I know that seems impossible because that is not normally how dreams happen. I somehow believe there are two possibilities and they are probably both possible at the same time. The first is that my mind and my conscience were so integrated with this thought that I couldn't think of anything else. My mind didn't allow anything else to come into it because I was so preoccupied with finding a solution. The other possibility was that God was driving those dreams and I would realize the true meaning when the time was right.

Here is how the dream ended so I could finally move on from it. The last dream that I had about this dam was one in which an older gentleman from the community came to it and brought some of the other older folks from the community. This may sound too simple but to me it meant so much. The older gentleman got up in front of the people that were gathered and related that the only way we were going to fix this problem was to do something besides just talk about it. He said there was no use in waiting on someone else to fix it. The government was not going to do it and the rich were not going to do it. He noted that if we want that dam fixed, we had to start at the source. He said that we should all get our old pickup trucks, wheel barrels, shovels, buckets and whatever else we had and every day we should go to the top of the dam on the inside where the lake was and start dumping rocks and gravel over the side. I knew this was not practical and it wasn't a real situation, but you see over time, he was right. We did as he suggested, and the leak started slowing. It may take years of one ton at a time to completely stop the leak, but collectively, we were going to solve the problem.

I realized from this dream much more than the dream itself. It somehow became very clear to me what God's plan was for me and how I was to proceed with it. I learned that the experience that I had accumulated over the years and the crazy ups and downs were all for a reason. I knew that it would revolve around the home design that I had been working on for several years but not just that. I could use that design as a primary product to be able to start a company from scratch that would have a more far reaching effect on this country than just building houses. We could segue this into a way to bring folks back into rural America and restore a way of life almost gone from our society. During all this dream process, I had been working day and night on these designs. I was always led away from the traditional stick-built homes and the large manufacturing process to which I had grown accustomed. When I explain the manufacturing process in the next chapter in detail you will see how everything pointed to this type of manufacturing and these dreams were so important in the way I looked at everything. I had to completely change everything I believed about start-up businesses, how to go about getting information out and how to raise capital.   From that night on my life changed. I quit looking for someone else to fix the situation that I knew was so important. I was spending all my time running to Washington, D. C. or to my home state capital in Charleston, and meeting with every economic development office I could to get the answers. After that night, the dreams were replaced with an actual thought process even while I slept. What a lesson to learn and it took so long to do it! I know it had to be done that way because if I was one thing, I was hardheaded. Several people tried to tell me that but of course I didn't listen. This change just took place over the past couple of years. After reflecting on this series of dreams, I realized that the major fault wasn't that I didn't listen to other people; the problem was that in the end I always did what I thought we should do. I never trusted any opinion other than mine. After looking back on my entire life, I realized that I not only didn't listen to other people, I really don't believe I ever trusted God. You could ask me how that was possible and how someone could believe that they knew more than God. Unfortunately, it is not that simple. I have said this before in my writings that God doesn't give you a road map or red lights going off with sirens and warnings. Sometimes He speaks in a small still voice and each person must be in a relationship with Him so that those signs or signals are powerful enough to get your attention. The most important lesson I learned is that God doesn't only involve me in his plans but also other people. I had to learn to trust that those other people are part of the same plan just like the older gentleman that came to the meeting and offered a plan other than mine.

Sometimes you must get a hit over the head with something to get your attention. I hope the last hit over my head took place about five years ago. I became totally obsessed with designing house from the ground up and building it. I picked our family camp at Renick as the location and I wanted to build my father a house to live in as he got older. It would be beautiful and very safe. I really wanted to build a house to prove that I could do it and to test a theory that I had on a different way to build a house. That design and the thinking behind it will all be explained in the next chapter. It was a very important design in this process that really made the whole business possible. As usual, I did some things in the wrong way and wish I could do lots of it over, but a person can only go forward. I will tell you that I went for another walk but this time I worried a lot of family and friends. I won't go into much detail about this walk, but I was driving around one day trying to figure out a solution to some very pressing problems that I had to solve. Again, I had made some monumental mistakes in some of the things I did and as usual, I was totally lost on what to do. It seems like you want to trust God until you really need Him. What makes it hard is that you weren't doing things the way God would have you to do them in the first place. I always wanted to do it on my time table and not on God's. That would be the last time it would ever happen!

    As I was driving, I found myself at one of my favorite places on this earth. I had just pulled into the parking lot at Cranberry Wilderness Area just out of Richwood and Marlinton West Virginia. It was late October and it wasn't that cold that day. I hadn't looked at the forecast for the next couple of days as I would normally do. I just wanted to start walking. I left the parking lot at the Visitor's Center and drove to the parking lot at the Upper Gate of Dogway Run, a place I had been many times. For some reason, I decided to walk down the Kennison Mountain Trail. I knew where it came out on the Cranberry River and I was going to walk down to the river and cross to a shelter that was located on the trail. As usual, I didn't tell anyone where I was going or that I was even going on a hike. My dad never really knew where I was and always said that he would see me when he saw me, so I didn't even think anyone would be looking for me. I did, however, tell a friend in Pennsylvania that I might be coming for a visit. Since I didn't show up and she couldn't reach me, she started calling everyone trying to find me. I can see why that happened but to make a long story a little shorter everyone was looking for me.

Besides the fact that everyone was worried and looking for me I was not in the best situation. All I can say is this was without a doubt the stupidest thing I had ever done. I was miles down into the Cranberry Wilderness Area with no provisions and just a small jacket and tennis shoes. There wouldn't have been a desperate problem if one thing hadn't happened. When I got to the exact location where I was heading, I had to cross a river that was usually well below knee deep, but it was been running nearly four feet high. I tried a couple times to cross the river, but I almost drowned each time. I think I was meant to stay on that side of the river for the night. It was close to dark by that time and it was a 10-mile hike back up the trail to the car. What made things even worse, it started to rain heavily. I know many probably thought that I went down there because I wanted to end my life. I will tell you this with all my heart; I never thought of killing myself. I was never afraid, and I told God that if it was my time to go I was ready and I left it up to Him. I also am not telling you all that was running through my head during that day. I had really made some very big mistakes and I didn't have the answer to how I was going to deal with those mistakes. That was what was on my mind that day and not my current situation. This has always been what I had done when I got into a bad situation, but this was the first time I got myself into a life or death possibility. As darkness fell, I realized that was a distinct possibility. I was never afraid of dying and I never have been, especially now.

There comes a point in your life when there is no good answer and I had to face the thought of spending the night in those woods that night no matter how cold it got or how much it rained. That was the darkest I had ever seen it. The area in which I found myself was heavily wooded and very steep. I did find one level spot and I lay down. It was still raining, and the temperature was probably in the thirties. I know you will probably not believe this, but I slept that night. I was laying in freezing water and when I woke up there was at least 3 inches of snow covering me. By the grace of God, I'm still here!

There is one thing that I really want to share with you. There was something that happened that night which I can never forget. I don't know if I was dreaming or if it was real. I believe it was real because I felt the snow on my face. A bright light was in my eyes and it almost felt like it was going to blind me. It was as if a car was heading right at me and I had to shield my eyes. It wasn't like a flashlight because it wasn't moving, it was just a light. I know at that time I felt warm and in a few minutes, I went back to sleep and was never cold the rest of the night. This was not the last time I would see something that I couldn't explain when I was in a precarious situation. Maybe no one else had any idea where I was but I know for sure God knew. I never told anyone about this when

I finally made it back to civilization. I never wanted to try to justify the mistakes I had made.

The next morning when I got up the situation had not changed. I still couldn't cross the river and I knew that the only thing I could do was to walk back up that steep trail to my car. I'm not sure why I always do these walks when I'm not in very good condition. The condition I'm in now it wouldn't be very hard, but at that time it seemed like a hundred miles. I had not eaten the day before and again I had nothing with me. I remember sitting there for some time trying to figure out what to do when I already knew there was only one answer to my situation, so I finally started walking. I don't know how many of you have ever walked the Kennison Mountain Trail, but I tell you it is very steep, and you must stay on the trail. The brush and vegetation on either side of the trail is very thick. I was so thirsty, so I sucked ice off the logs to get moisture. I was not traveling very fast because I stopped every little bit to rest and then I would go on. There was no way I could tell how far I had gone and how far I had to go. It was starting to get dark and I wasn't sure how I could stay on the trail. I was now concerned and very tired. Of course, I had no flashlight with me. I'm smarter than you might think; it just doesn't seem like it at this point in my story. One thing about being in the wilderness that is very important is that you must always be aware of your surroundings. The trail had very large mud holes that were now filled with snow and mud. I had lots of trouble keeping my tennis shoes on. On some occasions they would get stuck in the snow and I would have to dig them out.

MY THOUSAND MILE JOURNEY

Again, when it gets dark in that part of the country it gets extremely dark! I noticed that all along the trail every 50 feet there was a blue square metal sign on a tree that lined the trail. It was square with two of the points facing up and down. All the trails in the wilderness area are that way. Again, it was very important for me to stay on that trail. It was so dark that every few feet I would have to feel around until I found the right tree and felt that blue metal sign. The sign was only about four inches across, so it wasn't very easy. I also remembered that there was a place about a half a mile before the trail crossed another one and I needed to turn onto the trail to the right. God definitely guided me through that one for sure because I made the right choice! I reached the car about midnight that night and found that I had a flat tire and not much gas. I guess God wasn't ready for me to leave yet. I spent the second night in the car and couldn't run the heater or play the radio much because my gas level was too low, and I had no money. It didn't matter much because there was no gas station there. I did hear on the radio that the temperature was going to be down in the middle teens by morning. That night I got very cold!

 I did survive this ordeal and it was an experience that I hold dear to my heart because I learned from it and God helped bring me through it all. My family again helped me work out all the problems I had. One thing that meant the world to me was that I knew I had two fathers and they were both always with me. My earthly father was the greatest man I ever knew, and we had such a great relationship. My heavenly father held me in the palm of His hand. Change would be swift and constant from there on out. Patience and integrity were the two things that would guide the rest of my life.

CHAPTER 4

FOURTH WEEK - MANUFACTURING

The 4th week of my journey began on August 5th and what a beautiful day to get back on my bike! I was fortunate to be joined by a very good friend from my college days. We were also joined by a friend of hers that I just met on this trip. This is another great place to stop and put in a good word for the Greenbrier River Trail. This trail is in the Hall of Fame of trails for the entire United States and it really deserves it. It is a 1% grade over the nearly 78 miles and it's a great ride for any age person. We parked our cars at Beard, West Virginia and from there we traveled to Marlinton with our bikes. Then we rode back down to Beard. Along the way we stopped at a beautiful little convenience store/restaurant in Seebert, WV called Jack Horner's Corner. This is a beautiful little place right on the Trail with everything one could need, and they serve great food! I stopped there many times during my 1000-mile journey. When we got back to our cars in Beard I decided that I would ride back up to Seebert and have lunch there. I had a great turkey club and that became my sandwich of choice while riding the trail. The other thing that was so great about that place was that it was the only spot from Marlinton to

Renick that I could get phone service. As a matter a fact, that was the last and only phone service I could get going north. I never had phone service after Seebert from all the way to Cass and back. In Marlinton and Cass, I could get Wi-Fi but no phone service. That usually meant that I would spend a little more time at Jack Horner's Corner. With the trip back to the restaurant and then back to my car at Beard, my ride total was 34 miles. This ended up being a great day of riding and the joy of spending time with an old friend and making a new friend. We have ridden our bikes since and did some great hiking together. We will be friends for life and hopefully we will enjoy many more adventures on the trail and other places in the outdoors.

The next day I had some chores to do so I only rode 20 miles. That sounds funny that a man of 65 only rode 20 miles but I did catch up with two very dear friends on the trail that day and they asked me about my riding. They were following me on Facebook and I was able to share with them the joy I was having and how it was changing my life. I saw so many old friends and made new friends during my journey that it always made me smile. I always met them with a smile and tried to witness to them that it was through God's Will that I was able to make this journey.

The third day of that week was one of my very best days. I rode a total of 36 miles that day and it was the very best bear sighting day I had through my entire 1,000 miles. I saw one at the 30-mile marker as it crossed the road and then when I got to the 23-mile marker I had the rare privilege of seeing a mama bear with two beautiful little cubs. I enjoyed watching them because when their mom rose up on her hind legs the cubs will soon follow. They didn't look like they were over a foot tall but you couldn't tell them that! They looked so proud as they stood close to mama and seemed like her protector.

    The following day I had some things to do so I was only able to ride 10 miles but I had another awesome sighting! You see, I have spent my whole life in the outdoors and I have been able to see some of the most beautiful sights that this country has to offer. I have been able to visit 48 of the 50 states of the United States. The only two that I have not been to are California and Hawaii. I mean, I didn't just drive through these states, I visited them. The last two are on my bucket list and hopefully I will be able to do those this year.

    Keep in mind; this is just the day after I saw the mama bear and the two cubs. I was in the exact same spot at the 23-mile marker except I was riding in the opposite direction. Out in front of me about 20 feet ran this really big whitetail buck. He was so close and I was going pretty fast, so I had to stop. Within seconds another buck ran across the trail following the first one and that wasn't all; right behind him was the third buck and he was even bigger than the first two. For a second I thought that was the last one. Then out of the side of my eye, I noticed the last of four huge whitetail bucks as he ran within a few feet of me. The last was truly the largest whitetail buck I have ever seen! The thing that really set them apart was the fact that all four of those beautiful animals still had horns wrapped in velvet and in some places the velvet was stringing down where they had been scrapping it off. I was totally speechless at that moment and had to just set there for a few minutes. It was at a place where there was a big field, so I watched those magnificent creatures run until they were out of sight. I have been asked so many times if I took a picture. I do carry my iPhone with me and it has a great camera, but I usually don't have time to get it out. The other thing is that in those instances I believe when I try to take photos, I miss some of the sight itself trying to get the camera out. I have taken many beautiful pictures over the years and I very seldom get those pictures out and look at them but the ones that are forever planted in my mind are always ready for a quick upload. I feel I can see those bucks right in front of me while I sit here at the library and write another chapter in this book.

August 9th was the following day and I loaded my bike, Jenny Lynn, in my car and headed to Caldwell for my daily ride. I got to the lower parking place for the trail and unloaded my bike. That day I rode up to Anthony and back. I was taking it a little easy on this day because I had been planning my longest ride so far for the following day. This ride would bring the total for my journey to 405 miles.

This day would become a very important day for me, my journey, my book and my business. How could one day in the life of a 65-year-old person be so very important? I was going to attempt my longest ride of the journey and my entire life. Remember just a little over three weeks ago God gave me the vision to make this 1000-mile journey with no preparation or previous workouts. I hadn't ridden a bike in ten years and didn't even have one to ride. God helped me find the exact bike I wanted and there were no gears or hand brakes on this bike. It was a standard Huffy 26" men's bike. My dear friend, who helped me throughout this journey as my taxi service, took me to Cass and dropped me off. I was planning to ride back to my camp at Renick. Cass is at the 80.7-mile marker and my camp was at the 24.5-mile marker. That meant that the ride would be 56.2 miles and my previous best was 40 miles. I left the parking area at Cass at around 9:30 AM and started riding.

  I stopped about every 10 miles or so but I wouldn't get off my bike. It was quite warm that day and I had to sip some water each time I stopped. I only carried a few snacks with me but I did take lots of water. I would usually put a water bottle or two in the freezer overnight so that when I got to take a drink it would be somewhat cold. There are two water pumps on the upper section of the trail so I stopped at the lower one that is located at the 64-mile marker and refilled one of my bottles. The first time I stopped for a real break was when I got to Marlinton. They have a visitor's center right off the trail, so I went in for a few minutes to say hi and to use there Wi-Fi for a quick update. From there I went to Seebert and my favorite restaurant, Jack Horner's Corner and sat down to enjoy my usual turkey club and a cold Gatorade. I also let my friend that dropped me off know that I was fine, and I was going to rest a few minutes. I told her that I would call her when I got to Renick. I have lots of favorite places on the trail and one that I always look forward to is just after you pass the 34-mile marker going east on the trail. There is a nice rest place there and I have camped there many times. This place also has some great places to fish. I stopped there and rested for a few minutes and then headed on down to Renick. I was getting pretty tired by this time but I knew I only had about 10 miles to go. When I got to Renick I stopped by my neighbor's house for a few minutes. He gave me a cold water bottle out of the fridge and I sat down for a few minutes and told him about my trip that day. This person is a very good friend that I have known most of my life; we grew up close and we went to college together. He keeps up with all my crazy ideas and keeps up with me to make sure I get home okay. I try to tell him where I will be so if I don't show up at least he will know where to start looking. He is the one I called to come and get me when I was stuck in Cranberry Wilderness Area as I explained in the last chapter. Today I had ridden 56 miles and I was tired. I told him I was going down to my camp that was only a few hundred yards below his place and take the evening off. I had completed the longest day of my journey.

    I sat outside of my camper under the shelter and had a snack and took a power nap for about 20 minutes. When I woke up, I was feeling good and made a spur of the moment decision. It was about two and a half hours until dark and my friend had my car in White Sulphur Springs. I was planning on riding the rest of the way to Caldwell in the morning and she was going to pick me up there. I said decided to give it a shot. If I can't make it, I do have phone service in that direction and I can call her from Anthony or below and I knew she would come to get me. My bike is not the fastest bike out there because I can't change to a different gear for extra speed. The best I can usually do is about 10 mph on this trail and I had 21 ½ miles to go to get to Caldwell. I called my friend and told her what I was doing, and I told her I would call her when I was about five miles out. That would give her time to get to the parking area at Caldwell. I guess I got my second or third wind and I kept riding without stopping until I got to the parking lot at Caldwell. My friend was waiting there for me and I was so happy to see her. I could not have completed this journey without this great friend. The trail parking area at Caldwell is actually at the three-mile marker so from Cass to Caldwell is 77. 8 miles but I call it 78 miles. I had almost doubled my best day all in one day. I started this day's journey at 9:30 AM and it was now 8:30 PM so that meant other than a few short stops, I had pumped that bike for 11 hours because there is no place on that trail where you can coast your bike. It may be downhill but only by 1%. I was elated and I thanked God for giving me the strength to do it. That brought my total to 483 miles since July 15th and I was beginning to feel like I would make it much quicker that I had originally thought.

    The following day I finished off the first 500 miles with a 17-mile ride. I couldn't leave it at below 500 miles because I had to take a couple days off to do some things. I was beginning to get a really great following on Facebook. I am one person that truly loves Facebook because I can share so much with friends and they can share with me. Of course, I get tired of some of the mean political posts that are on there, but I can scroll past those. Those people have the right to share their opinions. The previous day I had 111 likes and 46 comments. I used all of that to fuel my journey and believe me it made a real difference! I have close to 1,000 friends and those are the folks that I am writing this book for and am working so hard on a business that will positively improve their lives. The other thing I wrote about when I got finished that day was that I was able to cook my entire dinner completely out of my garden. I really love to plant a garden and I love being able to enjoy the blessings that God gives me out of that garden. I was able to freeze or can much of my harvest and that really gives me a great feeling. One of the main things that we will be doing with our business is to bring back or add to existing family farms. We are not planning on becoming a competitor as much as a partner with local producers to help them bring their products to market. That will be fully covered in this chapter.

    The past chapters have been about the first couple weeks of my journey and my personal and business past that will help shape this startup company. Again, as each week passed, I spent the time on my bike thinking about each of these particular areas. Concentrating on each of these areas helped me put all my thoughts together in a particular pattern and kept my mind busy so that I wouldn't get bored with the journey. Believe me, I never once got bored! In this chapter I wrote about the third week of the 1000-mile journey. Now I want to cover the manufacturing part of this business. A business can't be started or continued unless it has something to sell or a service to perform. As far as that goes you even sell that service. We are going to be talking about a few of the most important products that we will be offering and how they will be manufactured.

    The first product is one that we have already had on the market and it proved to be a winner. The boat stabilizers that we manufactured between 2000 and 2003 were a really great product and should have never been taken off the market. The only reason that it was taken off the market was because I sold my patent rights to a company in Bedford, Pennsylvania and they started manufacturing them and paid me a commission for the rights to them. They sold them mostly through Cabala's and I actually still sold some through my website. I would purchase the stabilizers from them and sell them directly. They were very popular and would still be if we can get them back on the market. The reason they went off the market was because that company went out of business after 118 years. They made swing sets and other playground equipment but the competition from China and other overseas companies became too much for them to be able to compete so they just shut their doors. I was able to get all of the necessary tooling that belonged to me back except one item that was somewhere in one of their manufacturing locations in Canada. The pontoons were made out of plastic and they were formed in a roto molding machine much like plastic canoes or other large plastic parts. The molds that the manufacturing process uses to make these molds are very expensive. They are made of steel and have to be machined to exact tolerances and costs more money than I could ever raise personally. We have all of the sample parts and drawings needed to start producing including a partner that has the manufacturing capabilities to do this for us. The other item that we would produce in our outlying facilities would be the fully equipped small boats that are equipped with these stabilizers. They too were very successful but the shipping and delivery of these boats without a dealer network made it impossible to manufacturer these boats. The last part of this chapter when we talk about manufacturing facilities and their locations will supply you the full details of how this will now work very well now.

The next product that is very exciting is a raised garden-greenhouse combination that we will build and deliver directly to customers' homes. One of the areas that I have extensively researched is the market for family gardens that either grows vegetables, flowers or both. The Internet is full of kits and do-it-yourself projects that people can order and put together themselves or a kit of material that shows them what to buy and how to do it.

Before I go any further, let me explain one of the most important concepts of this whole business model. When America moved away from the small town and rural living way of living, it also moved away from being able to buy most of their larger items and have them delivered directly to their homes. Every community had people who specialized in various trades. Now there are still items that a person can have delivered directly to their homes and that is mainly because industries have not figured out how they can be delivered in pieces and assembled by customer. These items include appliances and some larger electronics. Most of your furniture is made in smaller pieces and then assembled in the store or at home. This is the main concept around being able to use cheaper labor from other countries. IKEA is a good example of a company that has really grown because they spent money on engineering to be able to make products that they could build in Southeast Asia and have they shipped to their stores and then directly to their customers. I'm not saying that this is necessarily a bad thing, I just think it would be nice to buy something at a decent price made from real wood and have it brought directly to your home and have it put together by the person that made it. The company also maintains it over the years. This concept will be explained repeatedly in this book.

    The vertical gardens would be designed to fit the customer's needs and fashioned to match their decor and the available space. Our company would come directly to the customer's home and not only assemble the vertical garden, they would furnish the soil, seeds and all the accessories necessary to grow a great garden but to also train that person to be able to consistently grow better and better gardens over the years. Our experts would be available to assist them with their needs. We would also teach them the best crops to grow for their area and what to do with their harvest by canning and freezing, etc. Too many of you that seem like overkill because we grew up doing these things and Grandma was there to teach us how to do these things. The sudden rise of companies like Whole Foods prove that naturally and organic foods are extremely popular and it's more convenient to buy food than it is to grow it. However, nothing is more satisfying than growing it yourself and storing it for those cold winter days. Doing it yourself also saves a lot of money. Another thing that I always like to mention is that the children of today have no real idea where their food comes from and spend little time learning because most of their parents don't know how to grow it. If you teach kids to get involved in growing their own food, they will learn the value of it. The economy is very good right now and money to buy food is there but that may not be the case in the future. I hope not, but these skills are something I learned as a small boy and continue to utilize as an adult. I built one of these vertical gardens and maintained it for a couple of years at my father's home in Rainelle, WV because we didn't have enough land for a traditional garden. I will never forget my dad going out to it on a sunny day with his salt shaker in hand and pulling tomatoes and cucumbers right off the vine and eating them.

    I mentioned the next item in the previous paragraph. I built an array of solid wood furniture from the log to the final product. I built chairs, tables, beds, stools, island counters and other beautiful items out of oak, cherry, poplar, walnut, hickory, maple and many more beautiful species of wood. The coolest thing was that most of the wood I used for these items was from trees that other folks paid me to cut down and haul. I took an excellent class at Virginia Tech a few years ago on how to build and maintain a solar kiln. I built one out of plywood and other items that were very inexpensive, and I was able to fill it with approximately 2,000 feet of lumber and without any heat other than the sun, I could have dry wood in just a few weeks. Solar drying of wood is the best way to insure top quality of hard or soft wood for furniture building. It does not dry so fast as to cause case hardening or cracking. One of the important reasons that I really like furniture to be built out of true wood instead of the way most furniture is built now is because it can withstand storms and floods. Most furniture on the market today is built by a process of chewing the log into sawdust, adding glue and heat then pressing it in a very large press until the glue sets. If you look at how God made a tree it is nothing but cellulose fiber, a living fiber, and glued together by natural glue called lignin. As I stated earlier in this book, I obtained an associate degree in paper making, much of which was about trees. It was about what trees are made of and the properties of all of the components. The lignin is an amazing product that only God could make. It is pliable enough so that it can bend and is so infused into the fiber of the tree that there is no chance of that any small section of that tree will be void of the exact amount of glue that it would need to last for thousands of years.

    We know that trees are the oldest living things on earth and they are still going! You are going to notice that most of the products that we will be manufacturing in our plants will be made from those trees. Even the vertical gardens that I talked about earlier will be made of wood. I made mine out of hemlock and that is one of our most beautiful trees. The problem is that in eastern North America we are losing most of our hemlock trees due to a small insect that was accidentally brought here from Asia. We need to use all of these trees while we still have the opportunity. The wood is beautiful and is used for siding of homes because if maintained, it will last many years. Another of my favorite trees, the ash tree, is also under threat from another insect brought over from Asia. That infestation threatens to destroy over 7,000,000,000 of the ash trees in our forests.

I could spend a whole book on the plight of trees. I could tell you what we must do to maintain the forests and to use all of our resources before they are destroyed. Many of you probably don't remember from your biology lessons in high school or college how photosynthesis works. Photosynthesis is a process used by plants and other organisms to convert light energy to chemical energy that can later be released to fuel an organism's activities. The waste material of photosynthesis is oxygen. Another of the gases that are taken in by vegetation is carbon dioxide. Simply put, trees take in carbon dioxide and expel oxygen. I am giving very simple explanations to very complex chemical reactions, but I implore you to study this from another source much more qualified than I. I am just using this to explain how our business has explored these areas and that most of our manufactured products and even our power supply will utilize our resources.

One of the other reactions that most people don't really understand is the effect decaying vegetation has on our environment and our air quality. I have no intention in getting into a discussion in this book about global warming and the effects of carbon dioxide on our atmosphere because that is a debate for another forum. It is a fact that too much carbon dioxide has a negative effect on our environment. I did state that trees take in carbon dioxide and produce oxygen but there is a point where the atmosphere contains too much carbon dioxide and the excess can't be turned into oxygen. It's possible that decaying vegetation sends nearly 90% of the yearly supply of carbon dioxide into the earth's atmosphere. I know that I am not an expert on these processes that I am touting in this book. I am just explaining the thought process we used in our manufacturing design and long-term planning.

During the last few years that I have been doing my research for this project I have spent many hours on the environmental aspects of business and the costs involved in all these processes. The prevailing opinion is if we can do it efficiently and make money, why not do it this way? Why should we not take advantage of everything available to us? Have you ever thought about how much lumber is wasted every day in this country and could be used for something instead of just letting it rot? For example, when Hurricane Sandy hit, New York City alone reported at least 10,000 trees were lost during that hurricane. New Jersey reported at least 113,000 trees had to be cleaned up just so that power could be restored. We are talking about a free source of needed inventory only if we design our company around the gathering and use of these raw materials. What we are trying to say here is that it is not only the right thing to do; it's the economical thing to do.

Now let's talk about the most important and most centric product that we will be manufacturing. I wrote earlier about a house that I built for my father in Renick, WV. I also said that it was a house I completely designed from start to finish. I spent several years working on a new way to build a house of any size that we would be able to manufacture for less than any house on the market. The idea and this dream began after the terrible devastation from Hurricane Katrina. This storm hit the Gulf Coast, especially New Orleans in 2005 while I was working at Tracker Boats. That storm left so many people homeless and it took the lives of over 1,800 people. It really made an impact on me because I met so many of the folks that were the hardest hit from the Lower 9th Ward of that city. In the years since Katrina, most of the city has recovered except for the Lower 9th Ward. Most of the developed areas of New Orleans have returned to at least 90% of the pre-hurricane population except the predominantly Afro-American neighborhoods. That area returned to about 37% population and most looks like something from a horror movie. Not only Hurricane Katrina but so many hurricanes, tornadoes, floods, fires and earthquakes have destroyed homes, killed people, destroyed businesses and caused billions of dollars' worth of damage. Yet we have done little to change how we construct buildings. Many of the changes that have been made by the International Building Code (IBC) have helped to improve some of the aspects needed to strengthen new buildings. I have a lot of respect for the IBC and what they are doing and I applaud their efforts. My efforts, however, have been focused on a completely new design that would require a much different way of thinking and will be the jumpstart of a whole new industry.

My research took me back in history to the beginning of home building in the United States. At first, I only looked at the single-family homes that were constructed mostly in rural Appalachia. Homes were mostly built by settlers as they moved west and on plots of ground that they were able to get from land grants or at a very low price. These individuals would clear their land and build their homes from the trees, mud, straw and whatever else they could find. Very little of the material was purchased. Skills were brought over from their homeland and passed down from generation to generation and town to town. These were very well built homes and many of them are still standing today. They usually started out with one big room and then added space as they could afford it or as the need increased because the family size was increasing. I know that there were other ways that homes were being built, especially in the cities along the coast, but these were the study group that I studied. Later, local saw mills helped with much of the material, so the traditional stick house became very popular. In the beginning, these homes were very well built. Most of them, especially in northern towns, used hardwood that was being cut and produced by the local saw mills. Local builders had all the skills that were required to complete the construction of a home. These skills included plumbing, electrical and finish work. Much of the work was performed by the owner, his wife and children. Many times neighbors would join in and help their neighbor family complete their homes.

I studied thousands of homes and how they were constructed and what materials they used. I looked at homes in the United States and many other countries of the world. I was in no hurry because I had a great job and no real idea when I might get started on another business. I wasn't sure that I ever wanted to start another business, especially in an area in which I had no expertise.

My research brought me to the conclusion that there are basically only four types of homes. I categorized them into the following: stick-built houses, mobile homes, double-wide trailers, and assembled homes.

Stick-Built Houses: The first and most common way to build a house is the stick-built style of construction. I define "stick built" as the process of furnishing the builder with a blueprint of the proposed dwelling and enough raw materials to complete it. Most of the materials are furnished in standard lengths and are measured and cut on site. Some things like roof trusses, windows, doors and other things are furnished complete. The homes could have different siding materials like brick, aluminum, metal, wood, cinder block and painted or stained to the customers' desire. Much of the material lays out in the weather until the crew needs it or in lots of cases, until inventory that needed to be there first finally arrives. Even though the building permit is obtained by a licensed builder, the actual person doing the framework of other important parts of the construction may work without supervision. I'm sure many of you have heard the saying "we will make that up in the finish work". I am not saying that all construction companies do this. I know many construction company owners and they have excellent workers and safeguards, but not all companies do.

Mobile Homes: The second way of obtaining a home is to go to sales lots and purchase one on wheels that has been manufactured in a plant. You would then buy a piece of property or rent a lot, clear it off and get some cinder blocks and have your home delivered. This type of a home is called a "mobile home" and is still very popular for those on a limited budget. My parents lived in one for a long time and they really liked it. The homes are not usually constructed out of the best material and are not expected to last for many years. They do have some advantages and the most common one is that they are less expensive. They can also be brought in and moved into very quickly or put back on their original wheels and moved to another location. That is the other reason for the term "mobile home". Unfortunately, they are not the safest form of housing. If they catch on fire, they don't take very long to be completely destroyed and they are not the best structure in wind. There are some real drawbacks besides longevity and safety issues too. The size of them is limited by width and length by the road on which they use to travel to their destination.

Double-Wide Trailer (Manufactured Home): The third type or construction category that I have investigated is closely related to the mobile home. As I previously stated, the mobile home is built in a factory and then positioned on wheels so that it can be transported to the potential buyer's property and placed on a foundation. The next category is called a "double-wide trailer", also known as a "manufactured home". In this type of construction, they are also made in a factory sometimes the same factories where they build mobile homes. The double-wide trailer is basically two mobile homes made to mirror each other. Both pieces are transported to the owner's property and set up. The sections are attached down the middle to make a mobile home that is twice the width of a traditional mobile home. For example, two 12' x 60' mobile homes when attached would become a 24' x 60' home. As the industry improved on these homes, the manufactured designs became even more complex and integral. These homes can now be purchased in two stories and can include many different sidings and roof types and can closely resemble the stick-home design. In many cases, these manufactured home builders use the same quality materials as do the stick home builders. FEMA traditionally used mobile homes for temporary housing in areas hit by natural disasters like floods and hurricanes. They have now been replaced by double-wide trailers.

There is an advantage to the manufactured home that is undeniable. They are built in a more controlled environment, and in most cases, the factory would have better support tooling and machines than hand tooling or small portable table saws and miter saws. The real disadvantages to this type of manufacturing is that so much care must go into the parts of the construction that comes together in the final assembly. They require very large cranes to be delivered to the property prior to the shipment of the large components. Any problems in shipping or just the normal bouncing and reshuffling of all the pieces can cause damage to the final product. (I have helped put some of these together and assembly seldom goes as planned.) They also tend to be quite expensive and many of their customers seem to experience problems over time. I am not an expert by any means. These are just observations that I have made in my research to help me to decide the best type and style of construction that I want to use in my overall design.

Assembled Home: The last category that I have identified is what I refer to as an "assembled home". The most common design that fits into this category is one I'm sure all of you are very familiar with and that is the "log home". A potential home buyer picks out a design that they like and place an order to a log home manufacturer. The manufacturer then delivers to that customer the necessary log pieces that are pre-cut and sized to be placed in a certain order that is within the directions supplied by the manufacturer. Normally the customer is required to install the foundation or have a contractor to build it and it must be built to the manufacturer's specifications, so the component logs will fit when they are delivered. I have also helped to assemble these kits on several occasions. You can also hire a construction company to do all the work from the foundation on up to move into a turn-key home.

The biggest advantage to this style of home is that they are beautiful, and they fit perfectly into a rural environment. Everyone seems to want a log home out in the country. I like them very much but that is not the type of house I want to produce in this business model. The internet is full of all kinds of assembled home designs and I have looked at most of them. Many of you have sent me everything could find on this topic and I really appreciate it. I also receive a lot of information on tiny homes and they are also very popular. Although I really like the concept behind the tiny homes, I do not want to get into building or manufacturing them. I feel that they are more like campers than homes. Take it from someone that lives in a 24' camper most of the year, I don't see that as a possibility for two or more people. Besides, there is so much competition for them that I'll let others build them. I have other plans!

Now let's discuss my final ideas for a home and the main product around which this whole business revolves. I picked the assembled home design and have spent many years building them and perfecting this design. The first assembled home I built was the one I built for my dad in Renick, WV. As background for this construction, I had designed and built two small cabins and a stick-built home. I never want to build another stick-built home. I originally designed this home to be 24' x 40' with two floors. The bottom floor was an open floor plan with a kitchen, dining room and living room. The second floor contained two bedrooms and a large bath.

The difficult thing about building a home at this location was that it was in a flood zone. Our family knew too well the problem the Greenbrier River has had with flooding. We had survived several small floods and then in November 1985 we had nearly 10 feet of water over our property. It was called the "Election Day Flood" because it hit on Election Day November 4, 1985. I had just built an 8' x 40' deck on the house trailer we had sitting on our property beside the river. I was elk hunting in Colorado when dad called me. Our trailer, including the deck, ended up a hundred yards below our camp wrapped around a tree. The Greenbrier River is the longest free-flowing river east of the Mississippi River. We had another big flood in 1996 and it seems like someone always calls them a "1,000 Year Flood". I'm here to tell you that a thousand years sometimes comes quite fast!

Because this house was going to be built in a flood plain, we were required to meet the flood plain construction guidelines set forth by the county. We had a close friend that was a surveyor. He set the height requirements and we made the decision to go about four feet higher. Each foot higher than the flood plain requirements meant a much lower cost for flood insurance. It also gave us some very useable space under the main house that could be used for a covered deck and also gave us a great place to work out of the weather. The bottom floor of the home would be about 10 feet above ground level. That made construction much more difficult but because of the design we made, it was not too difficult!

There are two people that I feel I should mention at this time but as I have said from the beginning, I will try not use names in this book. I am doing that out of respect for them.

They might get embarrassed because these are two of the best people I know in this earth. One is my co-designer and draftsman from Bedford, Pennsylvania and the other is my attorney from Richmond, Virginia. Let's put it this way, they are more "friends" than just a draftsman or an attorney because they haven't made much money over the past couple decades they have spent with this crazy guy! I do hope that changes soon because they really deserve it.

    We began construction in mid-2012 while I was working at The Greenbrier Resort in White Sulphur Springs, WV and I spent as much time as possible working on this project. We had decided to build the ground deck first along with the foundation supports. I will not try to explain every detail of this design, but I will explain enough so that you will be able to understand what we were trying to do. The foundation supports that we decided to use were treated timbers buried in the ground well below the freeze line and extended up. This design was approved and it is one of the most acceptable forms of foundation in a flood plain because it allows for adequate flow-through of water during a flood. The best example that I can give you is the homes that are built on the outer banks of North Carolina. These homes are built up to three floors and have withstood hurricanes and Nor'easters for many years.

    We had made the decision to use as much hardwood in this construction as possible, so I went to the local flooring plant and bought oak and maple from the stacks of lumber. They didn't meet the quality standards for flooring but we felt that they would be perfect for the deck of this house. The home was not dependent on this floor for support so only the people and the furniture on the deck would be of concern. My brother-in-law helped me get a portable saw mill, for which I am eternally grateful! Some of the neighbors offered to give me logs if I would go and cut down the trees and remove them from their property. I was mostly looking for red oak and poplar and we used the portable sawmill to turn the logs into usable boards. We also went to the local sawmill and bought fresh cut red oak and maple that still needed to be dried. When a log is cut into lumber the boards are still wet. They contain about 50% moisture. As I stated earlier, I had taken a class at Virginia Tech on how to build a solar kiln. (A kiln is a device or a container that is used to remove the moisture from any raw material.) In this case, we used the sun to dry these boards to acceptable moisture content. During a hot day the kiln could reach temperatures of well over 100 degrees Fahrenheit. I was working a full-time job, so drying time was really not a problem. While the wood was drying, I was spending available time turning the raw logs into lumber.

    In June 2012 our area and much of the Central Eastern part of American experienced a Derecho. A Derecho is a word that I had never heard in my entire life. I now know what it is. A Derecho is an in-line storm that has great straight-line winds. I had never seen such tree damage in my life as we had in just a few minutes! It stretched from New Jersey into North Carolina. I was working at The Greenbrier that night and it took me three hours to get home. That was only because I had a power saw in my car and I used it to cut down trees all the way home! The Greenbrier was just a week away from its annual golf tournament and they lost nearly 350 trees on the course that were over 300 years old. Luckily there was no damage at my camp and the only real problem was no power for almost two weeks. That didn't hurt my solar kiln and didn't stop me from sawing logs into lumber but it was really hot. Another brother-in-law came up and he helped me get the sawmill running and we figured out how to operate it. The other thing that this storm really helped us with was that a person who owned a large piece of land on top of a mountain close to Renick had so many trees down that he had a man come in with a much bigger potable sawmill than mine. They spent several months sawing logs into lumber. I was able to purchase that lumber at a great price and used it to build the house. One thing that I am so happy about is that a few years later our family was able to sell the house and this gentleman and his family was able to purchase it. It was only fitting since most of the lumber came off their land. I'm planning to build the third model just below this home so I get to see it every day. That family has been so wonderful to me that I can never thank them enough.

    To shorten the description of this design, I will say that all the parts of this house were built on the ground in 8' x 8' sections. (Visit our website and see the pictures and drawings to go along with my description: www.fourthteeliving.com.) In this design the full section was prebuilt and even the windows and siding was installed while it was on the ground. The sections were all bolted together with 5/8" steel bolts.

This house and the second house used pre-engineered bents that stood up; in this house every 8 feet and in the second house every 4 feet and the floors, walls and roof pieces were bolted to them. In both these houses the insulation, wiring, flooring, plumbing and interior walls were added after initial construction was completed. The first house ended up being two floors 24' x 56' at 2,500 square feet. The second was two floors at around 750 square feet.

    I hope you are starting to get the picture of this design. The third house is still under construction, but the design is completed. I would like to explain in detail the strengths of this design. This house is to be built utilizing completely pre-built sections that are so complete that even the insulation is pre-installed. Each piece is completely sealed and already has the exterior and interior walls with windows and doors. The floors and ceilings are also completely built and insulated with metal on the roof and the only thing that needs to be installed to the floor is the hardwood flooring that is pre-cut and will be put in place in a very short time. The electric comes in a kit that is pre-wired and drops from the top into place in minutes. The plumbing is also pre-done and snaps into place just as fast. No wiring or plumbing will transverse through the walls themselves; not even the 220 volt drops for the water heater and the range. The foundation is still the post in the ground but the connection to the house is much different. All of these units will be built on tables, complete jig in place. There is no need for any worker to have a tape measurer or a square of any kind. These workers will only have a drill for holes that are to be drilled by the holes in the jig itself. The only other thing that the assembler will have is glue and a battery drill. Each part is numbered and cataloged to match any others that would be built to meet those same specifications. They will all be built in a specially designed small factory with very stringent quality controls. When we receive orders, the necessary cataloged parts will be taken out of inventory and arranged on a trailer so that the first parts that are needed are the first ones off the truck. Each part or section is then put into place with a sealed strip between it and the adjoining piece. All of these pieces are then bolted together in a specific manner and a specific pattern. We decided to go with sprayed-on close cell foam at least 2-inches thick towards the outside to assure that the seal and all the pieces would be sealed to the next with a 4-inch wide seal. When bolted together they would insure integrity.

You may ask me why we go to this extent to make sure this home is water proof and that it is built this way. This is the most important part of this book and the reason that I found it important to write. Your home is the most expensive and most important thing that you and your family will ever buy. It is also the place where you should be able to feel the safest in times of disaster. If there is anything we should have learned since Hurricane Katrina is that it can happen anywhere and at any time. You are there and your precious children are asleep just a few feet away. We may not be able to build a house that is 100% safe at all times but we can do much better than we have been doing. We can also make it much easier and faster to repair if that tragedy comes. This is the first home that you can get on the phone and order replacement parts for floors, walls and roof that can be replaced in a short time and bring your home back to its original condition. For example, let's say a tree falls through one end. Normally you would have to find a contractor and in almost all cases this would be a major expense and take much time to complete the whole process. This house is designed with that in mind and we have already proved that this is possible. Although this house is not yet completed, we did build enough parts to make sure they work and the design preformed way beyond anything we could have imagined. These parts or sections can be built faster and less expensively than normal construction costs. The great thing about it is the fact that we can teach anyone how to make these. The home can also be put into place and actually moved to another location in a very short period of time at a very low cost. The first part you take off and put on the trailer is the last thing that you need to assemble. Even the electric, plumbing and built-in parts come apart very easily and together they can all be moved to the location. Also, a small family just starting out can buy a small house and add onto it as money becomes available and the family grows. The other thing I really like is that as the family grows the house grows and as the family gets smaller the house can get smaller! Take part of it and move it to the country for a country home or let the kids take it to college or start their family.

There are many parts to the manufacturing and we will discuss a few of them and why this design can be the most important center point to a very successful business plan. The first thing I would like to cover is how much we have to spend on manufacturing facilities. We are very fortunate that we were able to take the time to spend on this and other very important decisions that had to be made. The process that we will be using to make these parts or sections of these homes is extremely simple; we build a jig and that makes sure all of the sections are square and uniform and that all of the holes are drilled through pre-determined holes in the jig so that all are exactly the same. There is no need for any of our assembly line employees to have a tape measurer or even any previous experience in construction. We can train anyone on the job in just a few hours. It reminds me of the person that said he made cars his whole life and it turned out that he installed front passenger doors most of that time. That person didn't really build cars but he could take pride in every one that went off that floor. The other important piece of the manufacturing puzzle is the building that we need to build these sections is small and very inexpensive to build. We will be able to use any available space because we need very little power and none of the pieces that make up these sections are heavy. We do need storage room, however, because the raw materials coming in as well as the finished product need to be stored in a dry place. This is an extreme advantage when first coming to an area to start building. We can use any empty building with an open floor plan like an empty school, warehouse or even a retail location that doesn't seem to be a fit for any renter anymore until a permanent facility can be constructed. I have always eyed the closed and seemingly unusable former Magic

Mart location in Rainelle, WV. We could employ hundreds in that building! Take a quick look at other buildings in Rainelle, Marlinton, Rupert and so many more small towns in West Virginia and surrounding states. We could move into those spaces and create jobs and not even change the general footprint of the building itself. According to our business, we would want to move our manufacturing outside of town to create our own manufacturing site. The building could be turned back into another retail facility that would be much more attractive after we create jobs and bring people back to the area. This would be good for us and great for the community!

    The next area that we spent a lot of time on was the necessary inventory for building these houses and the many other items that we will be making. We built the first house of this design out of natural hardwood from trees we cut from local areas and purchases from local sawmills. That worked great for single homes, but it would not possibly work for a manufacturing plan that calls for thousands to be produced. There is no way that we could cut enough hardwood and spend the time and money required to build that many kilns to dry this lumber. We will still be growing, harvesting and drying large amounts of hardwoods and softwoods for our other products like furniture, vertical gardens and the finishing materials needed for these homes. During the design process we took this into consideration and the decision was made to try to use as many raw materials as we could from the big box stores like Lowes and Home Depot. That was very easy because of the extremely large amount of product lines and inventory items they have in stock. Also, this became so advantageous because of the amount and locations of their stores. Together they have over 4,300 stores and there is not a place in this country that I could find that was not serviced by at least one of these facilities. There are also many other chains and local stores that carry these materials. Why would we want to create an inventory and transportation system that even remotely matched what they can already do? We could not begin to try to do all of that and do it as cheaply and as professionally as they do. Also, by ordering the large amount of materials that we would be ordering we could get terrific discounts. The most important thing is that we can order the materials pre-cut or manufactured to our specifications. The less cutting or shaping we need to do on-site the better. Within this book, I will be covering much more on manufacturing; especially how it pertains to employees and very importantly, to the financing of this project. You will see that this is a many-faceted project and only really works when all the pieces and processes come together making an organization that will have multi-locations and rival some of the largest companies in the world. When you study how some of the great companies of today started and how they were transformed into giants, you will see that their beginnings were simple and had to start somewhere. Each of you can be a very important part of that beginning and an integral member of its growth.

    Before we leave this chapter on manufacturing, I want to share another very exciting aspect to these homes that will make them basically in a class all by themselves. Over the past couple decades totally off-grid housing has become more and more popular. Technology in the design and manufacturing of solar cells and breakthroughs in battery technology has made this lifestyle possible. Of course, the only real drawback is the high cost of converting your home exclusively to solar. Many people have added solar panels to aid in reducing their electric bills, but it is a totally different thing when you try to convert your entire home to solar. Right now, you can't even have a totally solar home built without hiring a separate contractor that has a special license to convert a new home to solar. As far as I know, we can become the only mass producer of a totally off-grid home. We have designed our roof panels to include built in solar cells and the off-grid model would come with the recommended wiring and engineered battery storage units. The other thing that is a drawback to converting your existing home to off-grid is that you can't take it with you and that is a major expense! It can cost over $20,000 to covert an existing home to solar. Our off-grid homes can be moved just like any other model.

    As you read the next two chapters, some of it may be hard to imagine. There are lots of details that need time to be proved. Please don't worry about that because this total plan took years to come together and it won't be totally revealed in just one book. The "how" and the "what" at this time is not nearly as important as the WHY.

CHAPTER 5

WEEK FIVE - EMPLOYEES AND GROWTH

My time riding and walking the Greenbrier River Trail and the time I have spent writing this book has been an experience that is beyond belief! The feeling coming from something so enjoyable is astounding. None of this could have been possible without reaching a totally different level of closeness with God and a belief that this vision was created by a power much higher than I. You may wonder how God can be part of a business enterprise and inspire its creation and arm its members with knowledge and understanding. I believe that the prosperity and comfort of His children are important to God. I believe that God has always helped those companies that did good in His eyes and understood that all things are possible through Him that created everything and that without Him nothing was ever created. His people need jobs, so they can send their children to school and to raise them in church to be God-fearing.

Week 5 of my journey began on August 12th and I did not ride that day. That was when I spent some time reaching out to my friends and family on social media explaining why I was riding and what the plan would be on this journey. I told my many Facebook followers of my plans to ride 922 miles and then walk the last 78 miles bringing me to a total of 1,000 miles. By this time, my conditioning had greatly improved and when you get accustomed to this level of physical activity your body becomes dependent on it. I was eager for the next ride and I had no desire to quit. I also told my friends that I would be writing this book; so many have followed this journey and their support became my fuel!

I also spent some time planning my activity for the week and I came up with a very vigorous schedule over the next three days. I wanted to spend as much time as I could on various upper sections of the trail because most of my rides throughout the years have been on the lower section. I previously mentioned that the Greenbrier River Trail has a 1% grade over the entire length of it. That doesn't seem like much of an incline unless you are riding several miles, especially considering the bike I was riding. Most riders could make up the difference with just changing one gear. As you know, the Jenny Lynn has no gears to change so whatever the grade my legs had to make up the difference. Therefore, riding up the trail was somewhat harder for me. I had ridden the entire trail from Cass to Caldwell in one day but I was sure that I could not ride the same trail from Caldwell to Cass. I did, however, want to ride the entire trail in that direction. I am not sure if you have ever noticed the difference direction makes when it comes to hiking or biking in the wilderness. The view that a person sees when traveling in a different direction changes their perspective. At the beginning of this book, I discussed the style of bike I had chosen. One of the main reasons that I made this decision was that I didn't want to accomplish this journey in a hurry and miss all that God wanted me to see. I wanted to take the necessary time to see all of the scenery, vegetation and wildlife and to enjoy the entire effect that it would have on me. Also, I hoped that I could share that with you. I really wanted to share this ride especially with those who may never be able to do it.

If I rode the entire trail from start to finish in both directions it would be a total ride of 156 miles. There is a bike club in Lewisburg, WV that does a round-trip ride in one day once a year. It takes from early morning to late that night and I'll tell you right now, I don't think I could ever do that on this bike! I made the decision that I would round-trip in three days instead.

Another thing I accomplished on that day and was to complete a full day of canning. As I mentioned earlier I really had a great garden this year. This was the first time that anyone had planted a full garden in this location, so it had to be tilled and readied for planting. The older gentleman that lived in this location for several years had planted a small garden there and I had helped him with it. He had done quite well so I figured that this was good ground and I knew that it should grow an exceptional garden. One thing that makes the ground so fertile here is that this area is susceptible to high water and when it floods it usually brings good top soil from upstream downstream and layers it continuously. I had an abundance of beautiful tomatoes and my green beans also did quite well. This was my first attempt at canning tomatoes. I was able to make five quarts and twelve pints, and I thought they were quite beautiful. I did have a problem that to this day I am not sure what happened. All of the jars sealed perfectly but over the next few days some of them came unsealed, so I lost about 30% of the tomatoes. I also canned one of my favorite things and that is dilly beans. I had planted four different types of green beans and they all did great. I planted Blue Lakes dilly beans because that is a straight bean and works well in canning.

    On Monday August 13th I loaded my bike in the trunk of my car and headed to Caldwell where the trail begins. I unloaded my bike and started riding. If I was going to complete this ride in three equal days I knew that I had to ride 52 miles each day. That also meant that the one-way part of each day's ride needed to be 26 miles. The trailhead is located at the 3-mile marker. I'm not sure why it doesn't start at mile one, but I guess the first three miles were never completed for some reason. This morning's ride would be the longest upgrade ride I had ever tried. I had ridden up 20 miles a couple of times and I recalled that it was not that easy. If I was to ride the needed 52 miles today that would mean that I had to ride to the 29-mile marker and back. That marker was past my camp and ended just below Horrock. There was a parking area close to that location, so I could park there and continue my journey there the next day. The other thing that I decided to do on this series of rides was to do the harder of the two directions first. That would mean that the easier of the two would be second because I did not want to face the harder part of the day when the sun was at full power. I have not spent much time on this subject but my entire journey was accomplished in two of the hottest months that we have: July and August.

I made the journey up to the 29-mile marker without many problems, so I turned around and started my way back to Caldwell. I didn't stop at my camp on the way up to 29 but I did stop on my way back for a snack and a time to rehydrate before my last 21 ½ miles back to my car. I have commented many times how great this trail is for those of you that would like to start a work-out regimen, but I can't express how blessed I am to have a place on the trail. I made the rest of the day's ride of 52 miles in about six hours and I was quite tired.

The following day I got up early and loaded my bike into the trunk of my car and headed back up to Horrock. I had just been there the day before but this time I headed up the trail and through the lower tunnel. I had gone less than a mile when I looked down the trail and saw a pretty large black object standing on the trail in front of me. I stopped about 50 yards from the object because I could see that it was another black bear and it didn't seem to be in a very big hurry. I am not afraid of black bears, but I give them their due respect. They are wild animals and I'm riding through their territory. In just a few minutes the bear just started up through the woods and I rode on. As I went by the location where it was I looked up into the forest and it was just walking up the hill and paid no attention to me whatsoever. I also ran upon a bunch of wild turkeys on the other side of the tunnel that scattered quickly as I approached. I rode through Beard and the prison at Denmar on to Seebert. As I rode past my favorite restaurant, Jack Horner's Corner, I wanted to stop but I made the decision that I would stop there on the way back down the trail instead.

When the trail crosses to the other side of the Greenbrier at the 48-mile marker I always stop to pick a few apples. There is a tree there that fed me many times during my journey. According to the mileage I needed to ride on this day, it would take me to the 55-mile marker. I would really rather park my car at the Marlinton trailhead the next day so I decided to go on to the 56-mile marker. This would give me 54 miles on this day and would only leave me 50 miles on the next day, but that was okay. I stopped to say hi to my friends at the Pocahontas County Visitors Center. I didn't stay long, so I got on my bike and headed back down the river. I may have been in a hurry because my mouth was watering for one of those great turkey clubs that Jack's had waiting for me! I did enjoy my time there because the food was always good, and the people were wonderful. I met so many people while I sat there and relaxed for a few minutes. I could also get my messages and send some texts to friends and let them know I was okay.

On my way up the trail that morning I had noticed some more Chicken of the Woods wild mushrooms and wanted to wait until my way back down to retrieve them. I wasn't sure they would still be there, but if another traveler saw them and decided to get them it was okay with me. As I got close to the site where I had seen them, I found that they were still there. Those mushrooms are quite visible from a distance because of their bright red color and they usually have a dark grey or black background made by the log where they grow. I always carried a small red backpack with water, tools and some snacks, but I always left a little room for a few wild mushroom or apples. I also knew that they would be my dinner for that evening. Fresh Chicken of the Woods rolled in flour and fried in olive oil is one of my favorite meals. I had also stopped on my way back and picked a few apples from my favorite tree to go with my mushrooms. I continued my ride back to my car and I was very happy to see it.

 The next day I loaded my trusty Jenny Lynn back into the trunk of my car and headed north on Route 219 to the beautiful little town of Marlinton, WV. Marlinton is the county seat of Pocahontas County and there is not a more beautiful little town! It used to be a very busy town during the lumber boom but like a lot of small towns, it has had its share of hard times since then. Pocahontas County is one of the first counties where I want to set up a manufacturing complex.

 When I got to the trail head at Marlinton, I unloaded my car and headed up the trail. I'm not sure if this is true or not but I do believe that the upper 1/3 of the trail is the steepest, especially east above Sharpe's Tunnel. If it's not the steepest section, it sure seems like it! The ride today was going to be a couple miles shorter because I went a little further on yesterday's ride. I began at the 56-mile marker and the most secluded part of the trail is from the 57-mile marker to Clover

Lick that is located around the 69-mile marker. I do love to ride this section of the trail. That morning was a very bright sunny morning that was so beautiful. As I approached the first of several large fields I looked across to the other side which was near the river bank. On the Greenbrier River Trail, a portion of the trail runs right beside the river and in other sections it is not in sight of the river and this was the case at this location. If you remember from the last chapter, I told you about the beautiful experience of seeing the four whitetail bucks in front of me. This was sort of the same situation except the large bucks were on the other side of that field and they were just standing all in a row. There were at least ten of them and some were very large. It wasn't a perfectly clear view because of the tree line that was directly in my site line but as I rode between the trees the view improved. They were probably 400 yards away and the sun was somewhat in my eyes but it was a picture that I will never forget. At the time I it looked like they were having their regular morning meeting, or another thought came to me from the movie "The Godfather". This was the meeting of all of the five families. I didn't want to disturb them, so I kept riding. I always felt reverence for the wildlife because I was riding through their home and I was merely a visitor there. When I got to Cass, I decided to take a little time and enjoy the area a little, so I had lunch in the little restaurant there. It was delightful and I even had an ice cream cone. They have some of the best ice cream you will ever find in that little country store. I didn't make it back to my car until nearly dark and that was okay because I have not had many better days. This was the third day in a row that I had ridden over 50 miles and half of that was upgrade. I traveled 78 miles up and 78 miles down adding up to 156 miles and two more complete full runs of the trail.

I took the next day off and went to the West Virginia State Fair in Fairlea, WV. On Friday of that week, I rode 16 miles and did the same on Saturday giving me a total of 740 miles with 182 miles left to ride and 78 miles to walk. At first I really didn't know if I could do it by the end of September and now it looked like I would be able to complete the entire journey before Labor Day. If you think it sounds like I am bragging, I'm not. I know this is only by the grace of God! He has allowed me to complete such a daunting task. The journey, the book and the business will be used to the Glory of my Father.

In the last chapter we talked about manufacturing and in this chapter, we will continue the conversation of manufacturing as it relates to the employees and staff. The second question everyone asks me after they ask where I am going to get the money to do all of this is where I am going to find enough people and train them. That is one of the areas that I really love to discuss. Our economy is very good right now and it seems like everywhere I travel throughout the state I see workers-for-hire signs that I didn't use to see. I know many contractors and they seem to be having a very hard time finding enough trained or trainable workers that are dependable; especially ones that can pass a drug test. We have spent a tremendous amount of time on this part of our business plan. Let's see if I can explain it in the detail it deserves.

I researched every employment philosophy that I could find to try to find the best one or a combination of ideas to complete my plan. The one that I spent the most time with is a company that began in the Basque region of Spain right after World War II by the name of Mondragon. I won't tell you the complete history of this company, but basically the idea started with a Catholic Priest that settled in the area in 1941. This was one of the poorest regions in Spain and had not yet recovered from the Spanish Civil War. In 1943 this priest started a trade school which became a training ground for managers, engineers and skilled labor for local companies.

The trade school birthed the first of many labor cooperatives. Europe had had its share of commercial cooperatives, but this was something totally new. This priest spent a life time teaching a form of humanism based on popularity and participation. I spent several years reading everything I could find about this company and I watched every video I could find and although I don't feel that this type of a business model is exactly what we want, I do believe parts of it will fit in well with our manufacturing and financial goals. It is so much easier to do it all when you start from scratch rather than trying to change years of past practices. This company grew from these humble beginnings to one of the largest companies in Spain with over 80,000 employees and total revenue of over 12 billion Euros. This is not a small company and it has always been an employee- owned cooperative. The first company they started began by making paraffin stoves that were in great demand after the war. The entire ownership came out of the technical school that the priest started. Mondragon now has a presence in the United States through their business model, including as the Cleveland Experiment. Several of the service companies surrounding the hospitals of Cleveland joined forces in an employee-ownership-corporation modeled after Mondragon. The time that I spent on research will be instrumental in the employment strategy that we will use in this business.

One of the things that I tried to do is pick products that required as little training as possible for the greatest return. That aided in the process of designing the products. The houses are the best example and I explained that design completely in the last chapter. We will still need many well-educated and experienced people in the traditional rolls such as legal, accounting, drafting and others. By stating that we want a work force that needs little training does not mean that we don't have a plan to move on in our company over time. I believe strongly in the education process and that is apparent in the amount of time that I have spent in classrooms. We will begin an apprentice school where all our employees will train. Many people don't have any idea what they are capable of doing or learning. It will not be a requirement that these potential employees have a certain amount of education such as a high school diploma or even a college degree, but we will look at all forms of education and determine the best path for their future educational needs. Much of the skilled or degreed work will be outsourced at first in such areas as bookkeeping etc. until we can find people with specific qualifications or we can train them. That is the usual way that most start-up business begins and our real goals in employment will begin almost immediately.

Last evening, I was trying so hard to put this difficult subject into context; I must admit that I was really struggling. There is so much I want you to know and I want so desperately to explain it correctly. Many times, during the years I have been working on this project and I wake up in the middle of the night with real answers to the best direction. Most of the time the answers are not always a roadmap of which way I should go but a very quiet voice. This time, I woke to a scripture passage from Revelation Chapter 21 where John was given a glimpse into heaven. This description is quite clear and beautiful. As I woke the words seemed to burst into my consciousness. "Behold; I saw a new heaven and a new earth" and I was trying to figure out what would be beneficial from that passage. I had read that passage so many times and I knew that there wasn't a literal reason that it was brought to my attention. Then, it hit me like a ton of bricks and I couldn't wait to get to the library to start sharing this with you in my book!

As I have been writing this book, I have never figured out when it would be the best time to introduce the readers to what this project will look like and how it will grow into a very large company. It is so important to me that its growth be not only successful but helpful to the people that need it most. In this chapter I will give you a glimpse into what a company like this will look like and how we will get there. We will look at our workforce and then, in the next chapter we will detail how we will pay for it and maintain it.

Several years ago, I started looking at how the population of the United States has changed since the year I was born; 1953. I also compared that to how much the population of West Virginia has changed over the same period of time. The United States population has doubled from 160 million in 1953 compared to 325 million today. West Virginia's population in 1953 was just under 1.7 million and today it's just over 2 million. That is a staggering amount of difference and Pocahontas was the county that I looked at the most closely. The population of Pocahontas County fluctuates at around 9,000 people and just over 9 people per square mile. These figures don't vary much over most of the eastern counties of West Virginia. I didn't really look at why this is and what factors caused it, I just wondered how we can bring business to these counties. This was not done just as a plan to help these counties; that's for other organizations. It was studied so we could see if there was an advantage to using these counties as a starting point of our company. If you take a serious look at these counties and evaluate their needs and what their possibilities could be, you must first consider the unlikely possibility of a very large corporation coming to Pocahontas County to start a business. The biggest problems would be the unavailability of an interstate highway system, the lack of technology and the lack of a trained or a trainable workforce. These are givens and not even debated, so what are the advantages? Lots of land and natural beauty really stand out but one of the greatest advantages I see is the distance from millions of people on the eastern seaboard. Now, we must consider how to take advantage of the good qualities and mitigate the negatives.

Since I began looking at this as a possibility, so much has changed. Great strides have been taken by the capitalists of the 20th century that this area didn't have at the close of the last century. For example, today no matter where you live in this country you can shop for the same products and merchandise as the person living in the largest cities across our nation. It can be delivered to your door just as easily as anyone living in downtown Charleston. The only thing that is lagging a little behind and is now quickly catching up is technology. Just last week there was an announcement that a very large fiber cable company had decided to bring a new fiber optic cable system through the middle of WV from west to east. There is also approval for over 6,000 low orbit satellites to go into service in the next few years. As the cities are getting more congested and less optimal for bringing up children, more young people are looking at an alternate place to raise their children. Also, more people want to retire in the mountains as opposed to the coast. The stars are aligned for a change and we can be the catalyst that starts the movement!

The first thing that we need to do is begin an in-depth study of available land for this project. I believe that we would need around 2,000 acres. We don't have to have all of it at first, but we need to know that it will be available as we grow. We would not ask the county to give it to us; we would purchase it but maybe the county could help with a low interest loan. I strongly believe that the government (local, state and federal) is out of money to give away. We also don't want to ask for little or no taxes because I believe that these counties need more revenue to build better schools and infra-structure. Too many times companies promise the world. Things tend to fail or they use their funds until they are all gone and then they move away. The land we would be looking for would be mostly timbered and without any infra-structure like power, sewer or roads. This is usually the less expensive of the large tracts of land and I have been looking at for some time. I want it this way for two reasons: the first is lower initial cost and the second and main reason is that we want to build on it in the way we see the future to be. Now please don't get me wrong, we don't believe that we will get 2,000 acres but that would be ideal and part of it can be in a long- term lease. Also, we would love to have something adjoining a national forest. I do feel that if a county is really interested in economic growth they will do whatever they can to assist us in finding the perfect place. These counties can cash in on tourism but that is not enough to fuel economic growth for an entire county population.

    The location that we would like to find would ideally be located not too far from the largest population center and the school system but that is not necessarily the biggest concern. I think these counties with low populations would really benefit from adding approximately 20 jobs immediately with the opportunity to add that many jobs or more each year after that for the next several years. Continued calculated growth would be better than an overnight boom in population that may come in and go away just as fast. Some of these jobs would come from the existing population and some would come from outside the area in families that would immediately have a job and be able to fit in very well with the surroundings. We would take great care in selecting those who join our organization.

    Now, let's review the reasons that we would like to have this much land. Let us first look at the power needs and how we are going to meet that extreme need. This acreage would not only be the site for our manufacturing, it will also be the place that our community will be built to house most of our employees and their families. Remember, we do build homes. With this much acreage we could plan for many years ahead and our growth would be much less of an overnight shock. We would like to be completely self-sufficient in the source of power; that means that we would have to produce enough power to do everything that we would need over the life of the facility. We believe that life will be on-going for centuries. This idea comes not only from years of research into manufacturing costs but also in the area of outside threats from natural disasters, terrorism, etc. I believe that one of the biggest threats we have is the possibility that anyone with a computer and the necessary skills could take down our grid. There are several rogue nations that already have the capability to do that. We don't do any of this as a form of isolationism; we do it as a community partnership. Let's look at how we can produce enough power to furnish all the electrical needs in a start-up and continue through an accelerated growth throughout the years. We have designed all our manufacturing facilities and homes and other needs to be as efficient as possible. Our first manufacturing facility will be totally solar and wind powered. Our first home would also be totally off-grid. Technology is in a very good place right now and I believe it will only get better in the future and we will be one of the driving forces behind this growth. I also believe that these are great steps to full energy independence, however, they alone can't keep up with the ever-increasing needs that our company and corporate partners that we attract to our industrial complex will need. We will talk about the other partners in the next chapter.

    Over the past several years, I have studied this area more than most and have concluded that we will be at the center of our community and they will allow us to do everything we need to do. Power that doesn't come from the sun or any other natural form is produced from the turning of a generator of some kind. That generator is turned by water power or in most cases; it is turned by steam as it moves through a turbine. That steam is made by boiling water to a very high temperature to well above the boiling point. The heating of that water in most cases is accomplished through the burning of fossil fuels like coal, oil or natural gas or through the fusion of atoms in a nuclear reactor. Our source will also use the burning of materials but in our case it would be through the burning of bio-mass fuels. I know you have heard of this but not in the exact way that we are considering it. Bio-fuels have really come a long way in the past several years but the technology for the actual implementation has not come as fast. Some of the drawbacks that have hampered the rise of the bio-fuel power generation are problems that won't exist in our situation. One of the reasons it has slowed is that the materials that are consumed in this system contain lots of moisture.

Let's first consider what bio-fuels are and what some of the materials used in bio-fuel power generation would be. Bio-fuel is simply a fuel derived from living matter. The leaves that fall off trees and plants in the fall, fallen trees, sawdust, vegetation left behind after clearcutting and much more are the materials used in a bio-fuel system. Although these are all natural fuels or fuels from the manufacturing of wood products, the major source for us would be the growing of bio-mass vegetation.

Now, getting back to the moisture content drawback that I brought up earlier allow me to explain how that moisture will not be an issue for us. Moisture alone is not a problem in the burning of this fuel because just by merely storing it for a short period of time it will reduce the moisture content enough to make a perfect fuel. A potential problem lies within the transportation of that moisture. There are no added BTUs to burning moisture, so the transportation cost is totally absorbed in the manufacturing cost of those fuels. This is not at all a problem when the burning of that fuel is within such a short distance from the source. We will discuss this much more in the next chapter when we talk about the financial aspects to this project but I'll give you some information here.

In the next chapter we will discuss the definition of carbon credits but let me say here that although the burning of bio-mass is a carbon product, it is not considered as bad for the environment as fossil fuels like coal. Bio-mass is made of stored energy from the sun by way of photosynthesis and it is renewable and any bad carbon that is ejected into the atmosphere is matched many times over by the regrowth of the bio-mass itself. In other words, we are improving the atmosphere much more than we are harming it. One other thing that I did not completely explain here (that will be explained in much greater detail in the next chapter) is the difference between bio-fuel and bio-mass. Bio-mass is the vegetation that we burn and bio-fuel is the fuel that we make from bio-mass. As an example, we can turn bio-mass into diesel fuel; we will be doing that. I will also explain in the next chapter how we can make extra money by growing bio-mass, even if we use it ourselves. That is accomplished by selling carbon credits to other companies. In short, companies like power companies that dispel lots of bad carbon into the atmosphere can buy carbon credits from companies that grow these materials. The management of this acreage and its forest and vegetation is one of the crowning aspects to those projects. Instead of allowing the decay of fallen vegetation, the acreage can become a great source for jobs and especially much-needed tax income to the county and state.

MY THOUSAND MILE JOURNEY

Another reason that we would like to have this much land is so we can grow vegetables and fruits to sell and deliver to other areas and to be used by all of the people in our community. I shouldn't have to say much about this business when you see what Amazon paid for Whole Foods. This is one of the hottest products out there right now and we can grow and ship to millions on the eastern seaboard. We will be much closer than most of the traditional farming areas. This part of the world has already proven to be a great place to grow just about everything and it could be delivered fresh daily. We could put together a network of farms in many counties in multiple states in a very short time period. We would also use this large amount of land to raise animals for use by us and also be able to sell directly to our members everywhere. Through our apprentice schools, these specialties will be taught to all our employees and the ones that wanted pursue those specialties would already be employed by us. We would train our own people to fill our positions; we would also use other resources for education, as needed. Our plan is to become great neighbors to all the famers and growers in each of our local areas by partnering with them and building large kitchens they can use. We will be giving them an outlet for their harvest and products that they *could be* making if they had some help. The possibilities are endless!

I hope now that you see my vision of what this community looks like. Please don't get the idea that this is a commune or some sort of religious compound. That has never been considered and there will be safeguards so that those things can never happen. We will never discriminate for any reason. We will be, hopefully, a great example!

Now for the next question and that is where in this world are you going to get all the employees that you will need for such a monstrous and ambitious dream? Jeff Bezos was asked that same question a few years ago and now they employ over a half a million people in the United States alone. Although unemployment is now quite low, I don't feel that it totally represents the available workforce in this country. One group of potential employees that would be a great fit into our organization is our veterans. The veterans have gone through some of the best physical and disciplinarily life experiences available to anyone. They are also trained in many different vocations. That training and discipline is often wasted in the years after leaving the military when they can't find jobs. They have untapped potential. I am not a veteran but I always feel that I really missed something in life that would have done me a great deal of good. My father was in World War II and went on shore at Normandy on D-Day. Many of my other family are veterans and I am proud of each one of them.

I believe that many of our veterans find it difficult to find work when they come home due to the relocation of jobs. When they graduated from high school, many of them joined the military because there were no other suitable alternatives available to them. The military offered a job, sometimes a bonus and the promise of college after they got out. They weren't guaranteed a job; they weren't told there may even be a job available after they got out of the military or even after they got out of college. This is not always the case but I'm looking at the numbers and how this relates to our business' future. Many of these men and women were sometimes very popular when they got out of school and had a lot of friends but that isn't the case when they are discharged from the military and move back to their home town. They return to find that their friends have moved somewhere else in order to find employment. That is often the case in rural America where jobs no longer exist and many have moved to other locations. The ones that remain sometimes become depressed and in too many cases, turn to drugs or crime. We want to offer an alternative to those individuals too.

    One of the drawings that are on our website is a drawing of our manufacturing plant that we will build at each one of these communities. The manufacturing area will be sufficient for making enough sections to be able to assemble one or more houses per day. As sales increase, we build more of these small manufacturing facilities. You will notice that in the back is classroom space, a kitchen and an upstairs. Also notice a dormitory set up to house those workers that want to stay on-site, both men and women. This is how we will bring in new employees from all over the country and train them on our procedures and more importantly, our total concept of manufacturing. As these people come in we are not necessarily saying that they have to move there forever. They, of course, can do that if they like it there and feel that is where they want to live and raise their children. But they can also learn our system and move back to their home area and do the same thing as they did here. This is how we grow our business to other areas of the country; by moving already trained managers to another part of the country to mirror the project they studied and help build new facilities. This time when they go back to their home town, they now become the ones doing the hiring and not the ones looking for a job. The military trains great people that built cities in other countries. I think we could use them in a much better way than we now do. I can't think of a place in this nation that we couldn't send these folks and start this type of a project; especially if the sales for these houses go half as well as we believe they will. One of our best sources for sales will be our own veterans that now have good jobs and terrific financing with a Veteran's Administration loan. We could even do this in urban America with all of the abandoned inner city areas that really need revitalization. It is already being done in Kansas City, Detroit and many other cities and is quite successful; but most of those are through non-profit organizations and they continually have trouble raising enough money to continue. There is a farm in Georgia that brings in veterans to do much of the work and they raise pigs and rabbits to sell. The most important thing that the veterans get in return is a place to live and a place that they feel like they belong.

    Another group that we are going to work with is the "under-employed" as we call them. Many young people that come out of high school are not sure of their future and they spend time working long hours for little pay in the fast food and retail industries. I'm not saying that is a bad thing. Those first jobs give them some much needed training that could really help them in future jobs. I love the McDonald's commercial that states that they are "a person's best first job". We don't plan to be in the business of stealing workers from other employers because that doesn't really help the situation; it makes things worse. When a new company moves in there is period of job bouncing. We really want to hire people that are looking for a future and to grow with us.

We also want to spend time working with the local schools, high schools, trade schools and junior colleges, etc. We will not try to get students to drop out of any of these schools because we like those that finish things, not those that quit. We also know that sometimes a person must drop out and we would carefully consider those reasons. I am a strong believer in part-time workers and I think that a great source of training for new employees is through part-time jobs because that time at our facility gives us a chance to evaluate them and also a chance for them to evaluate us. We understand that this is a two-way street and we would love it to be a great fit on all sides. I have also said that we will be initiating a comprehensive apprentice school that will teach every skill needed to be successful in all our departments, but we will also teach other skills that would be of benefit to many of these students.

There is an additional cross section of people that we want to include in our prospective employees and those are all those folks that have taken jobs outside of their field of study because there were no jobs available in their field. We want to hire as many as we can that have a passion for certain areas, for example; we will be looking for social workers and health and fitness personnel. Wellness will be at the forefront of all of our locations. We want all of our employees to have great healthcare, but we also feel that one of the most important aspects to healthcare is a great wellness program!

    Another subject we will be spending more time with is the Apprentice School and how that it will be used as an income stream and not just a way to train our employees. There is the possibility of attracting new start-up companies to our location and not merely building and operating our own facilities. Take, for instance, a person who has a new product that has amazing possibilities. I know that the inventor or creator will run into the same problems or hurdles that I have always faced. We already showed that our facility would be located with lots of space and would have its own power and infrastructure in place. Then, why not make it possible that others could come to our industrial site to perform their manufacturing? One of the major costs for a new manufacturer is always the human resources aspect of being in business; hiring people and getting them trained, along with providing their benefits. What would it be like if we could tell a prospective manufacturer that we can build your facility, furnish all of the tooling and even offer an already trained workforce? We will really explore this more in the next chapter.

    I know we have covered so much in this chapter and it all seems impossible, but I hope you slowly understand how it all comes into place. It starts very small with one location that could even be in an empty warehouse or closed retail facility. What I hope is that we have shown you is how quick and simple the growth could occur because we have taken the extra time to complete the roadmap for that expansion. Too many times everyone tells you that you have to start out small and there is nothing wrong with that except when sales exceed the facility or when the growth potential comes, everyone panics. In our situation that has already been considered and we are ready to execute. The next chapter will also add to the discussion and explain how the initial capital is raised and also how sufficient capital is maintained throughout the life of the company.

CHAPTER 6

WEEK 6 -FINIANCE AND MARKETING

I was able to finish week 5 of my journey on Saturday, August 18th with a 16-mile ride and then started out week 6 with a very impressive 52 miles! That meant that my total was now 740 miles. My body was starting to wear down a bit, but my enthusiasm was unwavering. The days are hot but fortunately for me the heat doesn't seem to bother me. I was really excited about the finale and decided to set a goal of trying to finish the walk on Labor Day. I had planned on taking a few days off before the walk so I could rest, however, those plans changed. I came home every day and visited friends that lived above me on the trail. We talked about the miles I rode and the unexpected surprises I encountered along the way. Those friends were such a blessing and their support was priceless.

The next day was August 20th. I wanted to avoid seeing the same scenery again, so I drove up to Seebert and parked my car for the day's ride. I didn't feel well that day and I didn't know how far I could go. I hoped that I could make it all the way to Sharpe's Tunnel, but I wasn't sure if I could do it. I rode 10 miles to Marlinton and stopped for a short time. I was just about to turn around and go back but for some unknown reason, I turned up the trail instead of down. I rode slowly for a few miles thinking at any time I would turn the bike around and head back to my car. It was up to me how far I would ride and there was no time table for me to finish, so it wasn't important to go all the way to the tunnel. I can't tell you how much I prayed along that trail; I never prayed for God to give me strength so that I could be looked upon as someone that did this great feat on my own. I prayed that He would tell me when I needed to go back. You see, when you are riding on the Greenbrier River Trail, you don't just stop any time and say, "I quit." You always have to ride back. There is no way to call a taxi and Uber doesn't have service there. Even if I made it to the tunnel, I would still have 20 miles to ride back to my car, but I continued to ride east towards Sharpe's Tunnel. I made it a little past the tunnel, so I could make it an even 20 miles from my car. I rested there for some time and it seemed like I got a second wind. That is actually a real thing that I have heard runners and athletes talk about and it's the point where your body gets a burst of energy. I'm not sure how that works; I just know that it does. On the days that I rode for six or more hours, it seemed like it came in threes or fours instead of just the second wind so that I could finish the ride. God is good!

    The other thing that really makes a difference is the change from riding up-grade to down-grade is remarkable. It is only 1%, but when you are that tired and pushing your heart and body to its limit, it really helps. When I got back to my car I had to stop by Jack Horner's Corner from some refreshment. Their turkey club and a Gatorade tasted so good! That ride added 40 more miles and brought my total to 780 miles. I did some math on how many miles I would need to ride the next few days so that I would have a total of 922 miles riding my bike. That would leave me 78 miles for my final walk. I knew I had 142 miles left. How was I going to finish those miles?

The next day was August 21st. I rode 20 miles and that brought my total to an even 800 miles. I didn't feel like I should press my luck and go for a very big number because of the way I had been feeling. By this time a 20-mile ride was kind of like resting a day. That was the number of miles I rode on the first day of this journey and I remember it was really hard! I was losing weight every day during this journey. I started out weighing 278 pounds and although I didn't weigh myself until the end of my journey, I went down four sizes in pants and five notches on my belt! My conditioning was improving, but I still had the walk ahead of me.

The following day was Wednesday, August 22nd and I had a dream the night before that I would ride the entire trail the day before the walk so that I could get a better idea of the camping areas and the watering places. I tried to pre-plan the amount of days and nights it would take for me to complete the full 78 miles. That meant that I would need to ride 44 miles on that day because I knew the next day the weather was going to be horrible. There was a 100% chance of rain the entire day Thursday, so I got up early on the 22nd and drove my car with

MY THOUSAND MILE JOURNEY

my bike in the trunk down to Caldwell. There was even a reason for that; it was so that I could finish up close to the Lewisburg Walmart where I could purchase the supplies I needed for my walk and not have to leave the camp on Thursday. Thursday was going to be my last day to rest until the 1000-mile journey would be completed.

The Caldwell Trailhead is the most western part of the trail. It begins at mile marker # 3 instead of #1, so I needed to ride up to the 25-mile marker and back to give me 44 miles for the day. The 25-mile marker is just above my camp and it's still in Renick. On this ride I decided to do ride the harder 22 miles up first thing in the morning and then do the second 22 miles back down-grade to finish the day. It was a very hot day and the lower section of the trail lacks shade. There is no water available to riders anywhere below the 28-mile marker because the area that was at the 13-mile marker was totally destroyed during the 2016 flood that hit Greenbrier County. There was a water pump there, but a huge rock slide destroyed the remaining amenities. It had not been replaced yet, but I heard money has been allocated to complete the much-needed up-grade to the trail system. Water was not really an issue because I usually carried all the water I needed to stay hydrated. I made it to Renick easily on this day and I was getting excited about finishing but I also felt some uneasiness about the upcoming walk. Riding a bike was one thing but a 78-mile walk is a different story! I rested for a while at my camp and had some lunch before I made my way back down the trail to my car. On the completion of those 44 miles my total had reached the magic number of 844 miles, leaving 156 miles to complete before I could say "journey complete" and "job well done". The 156 miles was important because that meant I had two times the length of the trail, 78 miles each, to make the necessary 1000 miles.

When I made it back to my car, I loaded my bike into the trunk and headed off to Walmart to get supplies. The supplies were for the walk. I used to backpack all the time when I was young, and it was normal for me to be gone for days at a time. I often went down to Cranberry or other places, but that had been a few years, so I didn't really know what to buy. (I'll talk about that more in the next chapter.) I spent the entire day Thursday resting. My body was tired, and I knew that the next few days would tell me a lot about myself and about this whole journey. I prayed many times that day. I asked God what He wanted me to do and I prayed for strength for my journey. I wondered if I was just doing this as an adventure and a way to get into better shape or if it would bring this whole vision to fruition.

On Friday, August 24th, I decided to ride the entire Greenbrier River Trail again from Cass to Caldwell in one day. My dear friend took me back up to Cass and dropped me off for the ride back. The first time I rode the entire trail I hadn't planned to do so. I was planning to just ride to my camp in one day and finish the last 22 miles the next day. I was planning on this occasion to ride the entire trail from the beginning. There is a little different thought process involved when doing it this way. I picked out different places to stop and rest. I also wanted to plan where the best places to try to reach each day on my walk were located. That was really a useless plan because I had no idea how far I could walk each day, so I finally just started riding and quit worrying about the walk. There are two good camping areas between Cass and Marlinton and they both have water pumps, so I knew I would spend at least one night at one of those. Something very unusual happened to me when I reached the 2nd of the two large camping areas and pump stations. I met a man there and we talked for some time. He had been there for three days because his feet were really hurting, and he had run out of food some time ago. He immediately witnessed to me in a very wonderful way. He seemed to know that I was coming. We talked for some time and I gave him all of the food I had because I knew I could get more in Marlinton or Seebert. When I was leaving, I told him that I would be back in two days because it was my goal to walk the entire trail and I knew it wouldn't be the next day. He prayed with me and I went on not knowing if I would ever see him again or even hear from him. I don't understand why but I had a feeling in my heart about this meeting and that this is what I was supposed to be doing. (I will talk about him much more in the next chapter.)

 I continued riding on to Marlinton and then to Seebert where I had my usual lunch. I rode on to my camp in Renick and stopped there to have some dinner before traveling to Caldwell. This time I rode the entire trail in about two hours less time than the previous one but it still took about nine hours. That is a very long day for an old man. Well, maybe

I'm not old but I was beginning to feel that way. I had finished 922 miles in 34 days of riding and all that was left was the final walk with God.

Before we continue, let's review the previous chapters. I think by now you understand what I'm doing in this book. I go through each week of my journey and then correspond that with stories about my life and my vision for the future. In chapter one, I wrote about the lead up and the first week of my journey and then I talked about the first years of my life through college. In the second chapter, I wrote about the second week of my journey, and about the early years of my adult life including all my work-related experiences that lead me to the point in my life that I could begin such a monumental undertaking. In the third chapter, I talked about taking a break from my journey to enjoy a much-needed time of togetherness with my wonderful sisters. Then I wrote about the time in my life when I took stock of my life and I went through a change in every aspect of my life. That helped make me what I am today. In the fourth chapter, I got back on my bike and continued my journey and then I explained much more about the business and especially the manufacturing sector of this business. Chapter five was spent on more of the bike journey and then I focused on the human resources aspect. I also spent a good deal of time on the growth plans that I foresee for this project.

In this the 6th chapter, I have written about the last few days of a ride that is on the list of greatest accomplishments of my entire life and in no way could have been done without the help and presence of God. In the balance of this chapter, I want to discuss another very important segment to this project and that is the finance and marketing part of it. I think this is the most important part because that has always been my nemeses in all of my business endeavors. This is always the hardest part of any business plan; how do we raise enough funds to launch and maintain the business over an extended period as to allow the business time to become profitable and sustainable on its own?

The financing of this business has been going on for a long period of time. Most start-up businesses must raise lots of cash for research and development to get to the final stages and ready for manufacturing to begin. That part of this business has been in progress for over 20 years now. It started back when we first designed and built the boats and stabilizers and then went on to the vertical gardens, furniture and homes. A couple of years ago, I built beautiful cutting boards and sold them to some friends and family and that allowed me to buy tooling and those folks are forever part of our business family. Also, there were people that invested in me and are still waiting for cabins that will be completed. I never forget one person that believed in me and I promise they will not be left behind in any way.

That brings me to the present and where we go from here. There is only one thing that we still need to do in the research area and that is to complete the last part of the home design. I have built enough of the parts and sections of the home to know that it all works the way it was designed. Now all that is left is to actually complete one model and that will be built on a dear friend's property in Renick where my camper is located at present time. The final design will be an approximately 800 square foot home on the Greenbrier River just below the first of three homes I built in that area. My sincere prayer is that the proceeds from this book will allow us to finish this much-needed project so that we can proceed to the next phase of the business plan. All the proceeds made from the sale and distribution of this book will go towards the finish of the model home and the initial start-up cost of the business. When you start reading this book much of that will already be completed and you can continue to follow this on our web page and social media. I plan for this book to be available on Amazon and other book outlets in early spring 2019. Following the release of the book, I plan to begin a very vigorous schedule of trade shows throughout the country. During that time, I plan on shaking hands with at least a 500,000 people and try to get them to purchase one of these books.

 Before I can go any further let me discuss with you another pillar of our financial plan and that is crowd-funding. Crowd-funding is something that I have been studying for several years. In my opinion, it's one of the greatest things I have seen but some aspects were just made available in the past couple of years. Crowd-funding is the practice of financing a project by raising large amounts of capital in small amounts from lots of people. "Kickstarter" and "Indiegogo" are currently two of the most popular sites. It is estimated that over

$34 billion dollars has been raised on crowd-funding platforms, mainly on the Internet. In most cases, the manufacturer or artist asks for donations. In many cases, they sell one or more of their proposed items before manufacturing even starts. I do not believe that this is always a good thing and I have researched several companies that did it this way. I have seen both good and bad. The biggest problem is that many orders and lots of cash comes in and then the company can't fill the orders because they didn't have a true grasp of the cost of manufacturing and the time period involved. In this situation, the person that contributed to the endeavor understood the risk and they just wanted to help get this project started; however, when a person purchases a product, they expect to receive it.

There is finally approval for the type of crowd-funding that we have been waiting on for such a long time. It is referred to as "equity crowd-funding". This type of crowd-funding was approved by Congress in 2015 and went into effect in 2016. In this book, I am only giving general information and the full prospectus will be made available well in advance of any investment opportunity. The idea behind this aspect of our business plan is to write the book that would be the roadmap of the business and give each person a history and a general understanding of the business and how all the parts came together. To give you a simple explanation of equity crowd-funding, I would say that most people don't really understand the stock market and how to invest in start-up companies. The Securities and Exchange Commission (SEC) is the government agency whose main purpose is to protect the investor; especially the non-accredited investor or the investor that doesn't have the experience needed to make an educated decision regarding the risk involved. Any investment opportunity that we would make to the general public will meet with all of the requirements of the SEC and follow all of the applicable rules and regulations.

I have a personal desire to allow many of the people I grew up with and have met over the years an opportunity to invest and reap the rewards of our success. I have never been offended by the amount of money an individual or segment of the population can attain but sometimes we need to level the playing field. The law says nothing about a person going into the local convenient store and purchasing lottery tickets that have little or no chance of paying out, but they have always been very protective of the same folks that want to invest their funds in a start-up company. I would much rather raise money a few dollars each from many people than to raise a large amount from just one or two folks that are already wealthy. These are the people that will become our workers and our customers in the future. Again, these are personal comments by the author of this book and in no way to be considered a legal document. I think we are a long way from any equity crowd-funding opportunities, but it is my hope that we can identify a large number of interested individuals when that time comes.

These two very important aspects of our capital raising efforts will be followed before any actual progress is made to pick permanent sites or begin manufacturing. That doesn't mean that we can't use temporary sites to begin some targeted manufacturing to help in the process. During this time, we will be working very hard on our website and social media presence. These are areas that we can get many more followers that we don't have the opportunity to meet in person and shake their hands. When we get the final model completed, we will proceed with one opportunity that I have always believed would be a no-brainer for our company. There is no other temporary housing available on the market today that better meets the requirement for FEMA! They are way behind on filling the need caused by multiple natural disasters in the past two years. That doesn't even take into account the potential of future storms. This is where our elected representatives can help us out. What a great kick in the pants it would be to have a substantial order from FEMA! We can go into manufacturing mode very quickly and release high quality products to fill their backlog. So many people have asked me why I am not pursuing that avenue more vigorously and I can only respond, "I cannot and will not until I can complete the last full scale model." That is not just for them, it is mostly for us so that we are sure how much time and money it takes to build these. Patience is a quality that I never had until now. The rate of growth will depend solely on the ability of our marketing team to generate sales. The great thing about this company and its growth potential is that growth is made simpler by the initial system that we are installing. We don't want to generate growth and debt; we want to generate growth through sales.

The other major market we want to hit immediately is a market that you may not consider. Look at the hurricanes that have hit the mainland of the continental United States since Hurricane Katrina all that damage. Now, look at all of those areas along the coastline that didn't get hit. When you watch the news outlets during and right after a hurricane, they pinpoint the most impacted areas and then they tell you about the lucky ones that just missed getting hit. If I lived in one of those areas I would be very thankful that the full brunt of the storm missed my home and property but I would still be concerned about the next time. According to FEMA, there are over 330,000 homes that could potentially be hit from a hurricane or Nor'easter.

In the last chapter, I am going to explain how I went through one of these disasters, so I know firsthand how it can affect you and your family. The worst thing that most don't see unless they go through it is the loss of familiarity in your life. That threatens your sanity and well-being. The place you lay your head at night can be stripped from you in the blink of an eye! It is not like moving or relocating; it's immediate! You could live for a time in a smaller place and you could get by for a period of time. We do it all the time when we remodel, but when a flood hits your home you can't live in the ruins of that house. It can be quite a long time depending on availability of contractors.

One of the major design possibilities that we looked at was how these homes would stand up to wind and flooding compared to other styles of homes. We believe that we can prove through testing that they will stand up better than most homes on the market in their price range. We added things to our design that will make them better suited for those conditions. They will all be built above current flood plains with adequate flow-through underneath and they will be close to but not part of the homeowner's main home. They can have a walkway connected to the main house, but it will be totally on its own and in as many cases as possible they will be totally self-sufficient with solar or wind power. These could be considered a "mother-in-law suite", a "man-cave" or just an extra room. All of these come with disaster relief amenities like escape hatches, emergency supplies of food and water, flashlights and many other things that a family would need in case they were trapped in this situation. We are not planning to build these and expect people to ignore evacuation warnings or take any chances. In some cases, time or severity is not forecasted. They will be built mostly as a place to come back to and a place to live while your main house is under repair. Try waiting on a FEMA trailer to come! Who knows how far from your home it will be and how long you will have to live there? This is a useable alternative so that you can plan ahead. Maybe you will never need it for that purpose but who cares? Everyone can use more space!

    If the first community that we build is successful and does the things we believe it will then full understanding will be apparent. Those counties and municipalities that we want to bring in as partners to help us launch these communities will be contacting us, I assure you. I have talked to so many people in rural counties and inner-city municipalities and they are searching desperately for an answer to these problems. The only real thing we are asking them for is some land that they probably don't see the immediate value of or some vacant buildings located in a place no one would ever want to live or start a business. If you wonder if those inner-city projects work, log onto the Internet and look at a few of them that are already successful. Look at "Urban Farming Guys" in Kansas City, for example. The people that were desperate and stole the copper out of some of those buildings are now the same people that they hired to put the copper back. Instead of feeling hopeless and alone, they are a part of something real. There are many more stories like this. We plan to work with those non-profit organizations to see if we can work with them as a for-profit partner.

One of the real problems that I would like to address is the one of banking. Most of the local banks today have been bought out by the larger banking institutions. They don't really work with the local businesses or individuals as well as most of the old local banks that knew everyone. You are just a credit score and nothing more to them. They tend to be more concerned with profits and bonuses for their executives rather than the communities or the families they service. Look at what happened in 2008 when Lehmann Brothers went bankrupt and the economy crashed. Those executives never lost their bonuses and now they are bigger than ever. If you want to study a real horror story, research what happened during the month of October 2008. If you can sleep after that you really missed some of the major parts dealing with how close we came to the fall of the world economy! We are still vulnerable.

Again, this is my book, and these are my opinions. These opinions are the thoughts that helped me piece together this plan. I am a very strong believer in credit unions. Earlier in this book, I wrote about the cooperative from the Basque region of Spain by the name of Mondragon. Mondragon expedited growth by starting their own employee-owned bank. In this country, we call them credit unions. To start the credit union, every member deposited personal money in the form of a membership fee then each of those members could place their personal funds in checking and savings accounts in that credit union. One of the major advantages is that the employee-owned credit unions can pay higher interest to it's' savings account holders than a more traditional bank. Locals flocked to Mondragon's bank because they weren't earning interest on their savings. Does that sound familiar to you? Before you start wondering if your money would be safe in this type of banking, it is just like the sale of securities discussed earlier in this chapter. A person or group of persons can't just go out and start a bank or a credit union. There are strict laws that are governed by the Federal Deposit Insurance Corporation (FDIC) to protect depositors. I know nothing about being a banker but there are plenty of excellent people that we can bring in to run this part of our organization.

I hope by now you can see how important this book is to the startup of this company. We need workers, customers, investors, members and prayer partners if we are to have any chance of being successful. Some of you know me and have for some time, but many of you are new to me and really don't know much about me. I hope this book will give you a better glimpse into my thoughts and ideas. The reason that I wanted to release this book and take extra time to explain in detail in my own words every part of this venture is because I believe this is sent by God to help individuals and families, especially those that struggle with poverty or drug abuse. There are so many other hurtles out there that make sometimes make life unbearable. I have no doubt that I was chosen to spend a good portion of my life doing this research and many sleepless nights putting all of this together. What I don't know is, if I'm the one that God has in mind to implement it all or just put it all together. Maybe there is someone else out there who can do it better. I know there are many that God will call to help, and I want each of you to know that I will embrace help and better ideas. Don't ever worry about making recommendations or giving me feedback.

CHAPTER 7

WEEK 7 – MY WALK WITH GOD

In the last few chapters I discussed the "what" and the "how" of the business dealing with my experience and my vision up to and including the nuts and bolts of the proposed organization. In this final chapter, we will deal with the most important part of our organization and that is the "why". Let's talk about the last 78 miles of my journey as I walked the entire Greenbrier River Trail.

I had ridden the first 922 miles on my bike enjoying the scenery and beauty of the trail. I also spent the time going over and over in my mind every aspect of this book concentrating each week on a different section or chapter of what I wanted to relate to you. This chapter deals only with this aspect of the journey and not the business. I saw things and felt things that to this day I can't fully explain.

On Friday August 24th I completed my second ride of the entire Greenbrier River Trail in one day. I began at Cass and continued on a nine-hour journey to the trailhead at Caldwell. That is a very long ride that drains all of your energy. I had hoped to get a day to rest in between the 78-mile ride and the beginning of my walk. The reason that the decision was made to start the next day instead of waiting was due to the weather.

That evening I went to the store and picked up the supplies I needed for my walk. When I got back to my camp that evening it was time to pack my backpack. I needed to get ready for my friend to meet at the trailhead at Caldwell because she was going to give me a ride back to Cass for the second day in a row. We were going to leave my car at Caldwell because I had no clue when I would reach that designation on my return walk. How many days was it going to take me? I had no idea. I had been an avid hiker and backpacker in my youth and into my early adult life. I became very good at picking the things I needed and was able to pack as light as possible. I knew I should only take the things that I would need to complete the hike. I also planned how long it would take and how many days I had to have provisions and the right kind of gear.

Thirty years ago, I was a fit young man. Now I was a 65-year-old that was overweight and tired from his previous 922 miles. Yes, I had a very difficult task in front of me. I had a nice backpack that my cousin left in the camper he had sold to me, so I laid it out on the bed and beside it I placed all the things that I had purchased to take on the last stretch of my journey. I had to pack my clothes, sleeping bag, rain gear and a blow-up mattress. I had purchased a blow-up mattress that would fit into the small one-man tent I had just purchased. I took a look at my bed and it was completely full of all the things that somehow had to fit into my small backpack. I started slowly and methodically to try to get all these items into each compartment. I stuffed as much as I could into the backpack but there was still a pile that didn't fit. I took everything back out and started over as I took away some of the things that I thought I could do without. So for the second time I started slowly to fill this bag. Again, I had some things left over so I had to do it for the third time. By now it was getting late and I really needed to get some rest so that I could be at Caldwell at 7:00 AM the next morning for my ride. At the completion of the last pack I had to be happy with it so I took extra care to not leave even a small space that I could stuff something in it. I got finished and then tried to put it on and I realized that it was too heavy, but I convinced myself that I could probably handle it. After I had ridden 922 miles, I had a false sense of strength and endurance. What I failed to realize was the difference between riding a bike and walking with a heavy backpack. I would soon find out the difference!

  My friend met me at Caldwell. I moved all the things that I would be taking on this walk over to her car and we began the hour drive from Caldwell to Cass. I was very nervous this trip. I wanted so much to be able to do this because I had such a great following of friends on Facebook and my neighbors were counting on me. I did not want to let them down, but my main worry was that I had felt so strongly that I was doing this journey because that is what God wanted me to do. I kept thinking of the possibility that I bit off more than I could chew. I just knew that I was going to embarrass

Him. I was having doubts that this was really a mission from God. As humans, we often have doubts when doing God's work. I had forgotten that it was not just my journey and that it was also God's journey and I knew when I started that I couldn't do this without His help. I was just looking at what I could do by myself. (You will soon find out that God made it very clear to me on the first night that I could not possibly finish this journey without him.)

  When we arrived at Cass, I start putting on my gear. My friend had to help me get the backpack onto my back. I had even brought a foldup chair to tie onto the back of the pack. I'll never forget how heavy it was, but I couldn't think of one thing that I could do without. I said goodbye to my friend and I started walking. I was still very nervous, and I didn't get very far until I started wondering if I turned around and hurried back, she would she still be there, and I could take the easy way out. Instead of walking the last 78 miles I could ride it in one day and it would still be 1000 miles but that would be giving up on what I had said I would do. To this day I believe that I was meant to walk the last 78 miles. As you read this chapter you will understand that this part of the journey was not at all about the "how" or the "what" of the business or my life; it was about the "why". This is my hardest chapter to write. It is so hard for me to put into words the things God revealed to me, but I'll try. I kept walking.

  I had ridden this part of the trail so many times. The first thing that really hit me was how long it took me to walk to the first mile marker. You would think that would be a given but the reality is much more striking. When riding my bike each mile marker seemed quite fast but when you are walking it seems to take forever. The first marker that you come upon first is the 80-mile marker and I was able to reach it without much problem, but it seemed like forever to get to the 79-mile marker. Once again, doubt entered my mind because I was not sure I could do this, but I kept walking. I could now feel the full weight of the load I was carrying on this trip. The first day of this final walk was all about me. I didn't spend much time praying or understanding that I needed to depend on God more. That would soon change.

    At first I was trying to figure out how far I could go that day before I stopped. I was a little too ambitious at first but that too would soon change. I got to Clover Lick and the 70-mile marker and I totally out of energy but that was not a good place to spend the night. I decided that I had to make it to the 69-mile marker where there was a camping area with a shelter and a water pump. That last mile of the first day seemed like ten. I was walking very slowly and it was getting kind of late. I kept thinking that the destination was just around the next turn of the trail. I had seen it so many times in the past few weeks but for some reason I couldn't remember the scenery close to this camping spot. Finally, I could see the bathroom facility ahead and I knew that I could get there. I walked into the camping area and could not wait to get this heavy pack off my back and sit down. There was only about an hour left before dark and I was thinking about building a fire because I brought all of the necessary tools and even some starter fluid to make the task much easier. I soon realized that it wasn't going to happen. I could hardly get up from my chair. Along the way, I had eaten only some things that I had brought that didn't need cooking for the walk. I had some protein bars and part of a sandwich I had packed so I was very hungry.

    The decision that I made in determining the meal for the first evening turned out to be a very big mistake! One of the problems that I have in all my fitness routines is that I don't drink enough water. I had some that day and although I wasn't really thirsty, I was somewhat dehydrated. I had to be because I had walked 12 miles on that first day and still had water left that I packed for that part of the trip. I had brought a small stove that burned a little square of solid fuel and that was the best decision I made. I would soon find out that building a fire every time I wanted to eat was not going to happen. I finally got enough energy to walk down to the water pump and retrieved some extra water. I drank some of it and the rest would be for my meal. I brought this dry soup mix that I just needed to boil water and pour it in for a few minutes and that's what I did. Of course I didn't read the directions or the contents. I did not even come close to adding enough water to the mixture. Too much soup and not enough water meant that the sodium content was way out of control. I really knew that but I wasn't thinking too clearly. I just wanted something in my stomach so I wolfed it down. I had purchased a blow up mattress to help make my bed a little softer and I quickly found out that it was a total waste of time. I didn't have enough energy to blow it up. Also, the small pup tent that I brought was something else that I didn't need that night because I was going to be sleeping in a three sided shelter. I knew that but I thought I would bring it just in case I had to sleep in a place that didn't have one.

    I just laid out my sleeping bag on the bench inside of the shelter and collapsed into a deep sleep before darkness even hit. I didn't even take time to thank God that night for helping me get to the shelter or to ask Him to help me through the rest of the trip. To this day I have no idea the time of night I awakened but I was so sick that I couldn't even find my flashlight. The darkness was thick, and I couldn't even see my hand in front of my face! My entire world was spinning at an unbelievable rate. I have never been so sick and just rolled over onto the floor of that shelter and started throwing up. I had no idea what had happened, and I remembered that all I had eaten was that soup. I was pretty sure that it was okay, but I was so sick. I was sweating and extremely dizzy, but I couldn't stand or even come close to finding my light or my phone for its' light or anything else. I had horrible dry heaves and I couldn't even continue to vomit. I had no cell service to call for help. That is when I started praying. I was miles away from everything, alone and in total darkness and I prayed to God out loud that if it was time for me to go, I was ready. I didn't even ask Him to rescue me. I really thought that I was having a heart attack or a major stroke. I was convinced that the end was near. I had never felt this bad. After lying in that same spot for what seemed like an eternity, I finally got up on my knees and was able to crawl a few feet to where I felt the opening in the shelter. I began trying to force myself to get all of what was making me so sick out of my body. After some time, I finally got it out and I mean all of it! I still couldn't get up, so I just collapsed onto the floor with no sleeping bag or blanket or anything else. I did have on sweatpants and a sweatshirt and with God's help (trust me, I realized it was with His help) I feel asleep. I firmly believe, and always will, that I didn't fall asleep because I was so tired. I feel asleep because God allowed me to sleep because I needed the rest and He had already given me the lesson that I so desperately needed.

When I woke the next morning there was a slight rain falling and I was very cold, but I felt so much better I didn't care at all about the cold or the rain. The shelter needed some cleaning. I did that the best I could and that helped me warm up my body. I gathered my things but first I got on my knees and started talking to God. As soon as I awoke, I knew exactly what the message was that He wanted me to understand. I had brought way too much gear and things that I felt I needed just in case. I didn't realize that God had my back and He wouldn't let anything happen to me. That was the first major lesson that I would learn on this walk that would change my life forever. I had brought a large trash bag with me and as soon as I finished praying, I started filling it up with the things that I didn't really need. The first thing I didn't need was the small pup tent, so it went into the bag. The next thing was the heavy air mattress that I knew I could do without, so it went into the bag. The foldup chair was next because although it was a little more comfortable than a bench, it wasn't worth carrying 66 more miles. The hatchet went next because I realized starting campfires was not going to be on my list of things to do. Some more extra clothes and a few other things were stuffed into the bag and I took it into the woods and covered it up. I knew that I could come back and get it on my bike another day. If someone found it and could use it, they could have it because it wasn't worth my life. That lesson was the only reason that I was able to complete the walk. That is why the title of this chapter is called "My Walk with God" because there was never another moment of this trip that He wasn't the focus. After that I knew I could do it and the doubt never returned. That is the lesson for my life's journey; it may not be easy and roadblocks will still come, but I know with His help I can do it!

The next day was Sunday, August 25th and I started down the road on the second day of my walk with God. It was lightly raining, so I put on the light poncho I brought with me that covered me and my backpack. It was truly amazing how good I felt considering the night I had experienced. I was now 12 miles in of my 78-mile walk leaving me 66 miles to go. I wondered how far I should go that day. I wanted to go at least to Marlinton or a mile below it to the 55-mile marker. That would be a total of 14 miles for the second day. I wanted to go further but I needed to at least go to that spot, so I could have cover over me that night. I didn't eat anything before I left because my stomach was still feeling a little upset but I did carry some high protein drinks that I drank on the way that gave me some needed energy, so I was good. One of my favorite spots was at the 67-mile marker so I stopped there and enjoyed the drink and some more of my trail mix. I had some instant oat meal with me but I thought I would wait and boil some water for that later. I spent the whole morning thinking about the events of the previous night and the more I thought about it the more I understood how important it was that God was with me. Messages from God were not over for the day and as a matter of fact, they were just beginning.

Just below the 67-mile marker is the longest straight stretch on the trail. It was nearly a mile long and I remember walking down that trail for what seemed like forever to get to the next mile marker. The end of that stretch was close to the upper tunnel and I stopped to rest there for a bit. That was the point at which the trail crossed to the other side of the river. The next several miles were more secluded than the previous part of the trail. I got up and started walking again and I knew that at the 64-mile marker was the location of the next water pump so I could get some more water. I was trying to consume more water than the previous day, so I wouldn't get so dehydrated. As I approached that marker I saw someone standing in the road as if they were waiting for me. I didn't know for sure but I thought maybe it was the man that I had met two days earlier on my ride but he was supposed to be well on his way. As I got closer I realized that it was him and that he was truly waiting for me to get there. Everything he had was packed and ready to go and he greeted me and still remembered my name. I followed him down to the shelter where he had been staying the last 5 days. He still had no food except for the few things that other travelers had given him, so

I ask him why he continued to stay at that spot. He said God told him to wait for me. We sat down and I started my little portable stove and made us both some instant oat meal and we enjoyed it together as we talked. Before I go any farther, I must say that I still don't understand this event in my life and some I have told this story say that he was an angel sent by God. I'm still not sure. All that I know is that this was truly a man of God and I was about to get a real education in all things biblical.

    I shared more of the food that I had brought with him because I knew I could replace these things in Marlinton and I was happy to share. We talked for about an hour and he had previously decided that he would walk with me for a few miles until we reached another shelter about six miles on down the trail. I was planning to go on to at least the 55-mile marker. His destination was Marlinton where he had friends to visit.

    As we continued our walk down the trail I was amazed at the things he shared with me. He knew the Bible inside and out! I never met anyone that could quote as much scripture at the perfect time from both the Old and New Testaments until I met him. He could quote several verses at a time just when I needed to hear them. He was not trying to preach to me and he had no doubt that I was saved and that I was on a mission from God. He was sent to give me encouragement for that mission. He knew I had always struggled with prayer and how to pray and why sometimes I felt that God didn't answer all the prayers. He looked at me and told me that he knew I had always drifted between happiness and unhappiness, so he explained to me using scripture the true meaning of joy and the difference between happiness and joy. I guarantee you there is a huge difference and now it was clear. We stopped along the way to enjoy wild apples and made a feast of tame grapes and wild grapes. I had not seen any of these on my many bike rides because I was moving too fast. Sometimes we need to slow down to appreciate God's bounty.

We finally reached the place where he had intended to stay, and we sat on the bench and talked a little more. As I got up to leave, he reached into his pocket and pulled out a quarter and gave it. He quoted a bible scripture and told me that I should leave with each person I met along the trail something that would be proof of the meeting. The amazing thing was that early that morning when I was getting ready to leave the shelter that I had been so sick in the previous night there was a quarter by my things. I knew it wasn't mine, but I picked it up and put it in my pocket. At the same time this man gave me the quarter and quoted the scripture I reached back into my pocket and I gave him the quarter I had found that morning. I'm not sure yet what it means but it was a great moment. He prayed, and I left thinking this would be the last time I would see him. As I walked towards Marlinton, I talked with God and asked him to help me out with this and calm came over me and I felt that I was not really to question just appreciate it and I did.

When I reached Marlinton, I had to walk about a half a mile to try to find some Band-Aids for my blistered feet. You would think after packing so much stuff I would have at least thought of packing some Band-Aids. There was a Subway at the convenience store, so I decided to buy a large sub and take it with me to eat at my destination for the day. Of course, they had no bandages at this store but a wonderful young lady that worked there gave me four out of her purse. That was so kind of her and after I got my sub and got some change I wanted to give her some money for them but she had left for the day. She actually gave them to me as she was leaving and I didn't know that. (I have stopped in there since then, but I still haven't seen her. If you ever read this book and realize that it was you, please contact me. You are amazing.)

    I left there and walked back to the trail and then another mile to the local park that allowed campers to spend the night in the picnic shelters. I sat down on the picnic bench and started eating my Subway sandwich that I had just bought along with a large Power-Aid and that really tasted good. I was only able to eat half of it because it seems that walking 14 miles carrying a backpack doesn't leave you with too much of an appetite. You would think it would, but I probably lost 15 pounds on this walk. I was very tired and a little sleepy because I really hadn't slept much the previous night, so I rolled out my sleeping bag on a picnic table with the intention of taking a nap. As I lay there looking back over the road I came in on as it was now nearly dark, I noticed someone walking my way. It was my friend from earlier that had decided to come on to Marlinton that night instead of the next morning. I had not told him where I was going to stop, and this was a mile past where he was going. I don't pretend to understand why but our paths crossed again. I do think I know but I'll let you decide. I had food left over because I couldn't eat the other half of my sub and I knew it wouldn't be good the next day, so he had that for dinner. It was as if we hadn't parted earlier because he began right where he left off and I was truly amazed how much everything he said was something I needed to hear. He talked a lot about the Apostle Paul but spent much of his time talking about Mark. Mark was someone that I had never really studied much, and he did such a wonderful job talking about the Old Testament and relating it to the New Testament. That is something I never even thought about before but now I do. We talked into the night and then I got a great night's sleep. The next morning, I got up and said goodbye as he remained in bed. I didn't set out on this walk expecting to get a lesson from God on trusting Him and I didn't expect to meet a real man of God that would give me more understanding in God's ways than all the training I had received in my previous years. For those things I am eternally grateful and my life will never be the same. I have never heard from that man again and I don't even know if he really existed with the name he gave me. It really doesn't matter because if God wants me to hear from him again I will.

At that point I had walked a total of 26 miles. That left me 52 remaining miles. I needed to get a little more distance completed that day towards my destination. I didn't get much food in Marlinton because I knew that Seebert was well within my reach and my favorite restaurant and general store was there. I had a nine mile walk to get there so I was moving down the trail at a good pace and stopped at another favorite place before reaching the store. It is at the 48-mile marker at the trestle that moves the trail back to the other side of the river. The reason I like that place is because it is the first place that I can get phone service. I hadn't sent a message to anyone in three days and although I enjoyed it, I am a creature of habit and like most people I am tied to my phone. I also ran into a good friend from Seebert that rides the trail every day. That day was no different. I am not putting names in this book, but he will know who I am talking about when he reads this. I have really enjoyed talking to him and we have now become friends on Facebook and stay in contact.

    I finally reached the restaurant and sat down for a while to enjoy my usual turkey club and a cold drink. When I finished dining, I was on my way. I wanted to try to get at least to the 40-mile marker because there was a little camping area there and that was four more miles. One of the things that I haven't talked about yet was the mosquitoes. They weren't a bother when riding a bike because you were going too fast for them to bother you. That is not the case when you are walking! That camping area was too close to a stream where the mosquito population was heavy, so I kept moving. As I walked, I used a maple branch covered with leaves so I could swat them. I actually moved it back and forward in front of my face as I walked.

    I reached Beard and that was at the 38 ½-mile marker and then another problem popped up. I was running out of water and there was no pump until the 28-mile marker. Yes, I know that all of you backpackers will ask why I didn't take a water purifier of some kind. Well I didn't and now I wasn't sure what I should do. I went over to the river and got some water and brought out my little stove and boiled it. I did figure out one thing that made the warm water more drinkable. I used those little instant coffee packets that I brought and made coffee. That worked quite well because warm drinks get into your system much faster than something cold. There was no good place there to sleep for the night where I could escape the bugs, so I decided to go on to the next camping area that was located just below the 34-mile marker. I started out at the 55-mile marker so that would give me 21 miles for the day and I wasn't sure I could do it, but I wanted to try. Stopping anywhere along the way would be just as good as where I was at this time so why not? Physically I thought I could do it but my feet were getting much worse with every mile. I was trying to be as gentle on them as I could but what could I do? I just kept walking. My relationship with God really helped me to keep going because my mind stayed so occupied on the things that I had learned. Things had become clear to me. The first day of this walk was hard because I just thought about the load I was carrying, and I didn't know if I could even make it. Now I had a bigger purpose and I knew I could make it but I wasn't sure how long it would take me. As it turns out, that really doesn't matter as long as I am in the center of God's will.

When I got closer to the destination point that I wanted to achieve for the day it began to get dark. I had brought a small flashlight, but the moon was so bright that I didn't need it. That was an amazing three miles as I walked the trail by moonlight. So many have asked me if I was afraid. Never for a minute did I question the walk in the dark and just being able to trust someone much bigger than me. He would get me there and if it was meant for me to meet something in the dark then that would be okay too. You see one of the things that this man of God helped me to understand was that prayer is a three-part process. The first is that prayer is a continual thing. That means that you don't just wait until something happens or you want something and then you find time to pray. The second is that we should live a life of prayer and that means that we should always be in the right situation that we would feel completely comfortable going to God anywhere and anytime. The third is that we should always be ready to accept God's answer to our prayers, whatever it is. As I got closer to the spot that I had been to many times I got excited to see it and not only because I was so tired. I was excited that I was able to walk 21 miles that day and I was still going. After that first day I never thought that would be possible. I went on a few hundred yards to my friends' camp and slept on their porch. I wondered why there were no bugs there and in the morning I soon found out why. I have never seen so many bats in the sky as I saw that morning. Those bats were feasting on all the bugs and there were none left to feast on me!

Day four was Tuesday, August 28th and I only planned on walking to my camp about 10 miles away. That next 10 miles turned out to be a very long way because when I got up that morning my feet were blistered and bleeding and I had no more clean socks so all the sweat from the previous day was grinding on my feet. Another thing I probably didn't mention was that the surface of this trail was small cinders and gravel. It was like walking on sandpaper and they continued to get inside of my shoes. I would have to stop every little bit to get them out. I made it to my camp in the early afternoon and was able for the first time rest in a very comfortable chair. It seemed like I sat in that chair for an hour before I even thought about getting up. I took my shoes off and let my feet breathe for a while and then soaked them in hot water. One of my neighbors came down to check on me. When I showed him the bottom of my feet he had to turn away. He said I needed to wait a few days before trying to finish my walk, but I knew then that I was going to go ahead and go back to walking the trail the next day.

That night I was really looking forward to sleeping in my own bed and I had a bed in that camper that I really enjoyed. It seemed like that was my worst night's sleep except for the first night when I was so sick. I could not go to sleep because I kept thinking about the walk I had the next day. During the 922 mile ride I posted nearly every day about my ride and all of the experiences along the way. For some reason I posted very little about this walk because it was between God and myself and I could tell everyone about it later. With the bike rides I could plan how far I would ride and announce it to my friends and I was always able to meet it or even exceed it but this was different. I was worried about my feet and in this case it wasn't that I didn't trust God because we had been able to do that. The problem was in me trying to figure how far I should try to go and how fast. I told you before that God doesn't give you a cheat sheet, so you can figure out the best plan, so I prayed a lot that night.

My camp is at the 24 ½ mile marker and the car was sitting at the 3-mile marker in Caldwell. That meant there were 21 ½ miles between me and my car and was I going to try to do it in one or two days. Logistically it would be easier to do it in one day because I didn't have to involve anyone else. If I would do it in two days someone would have to pick me up in Anthony and bring me home and back to Anthony the next day, so I could finish. I decided that I would make that decision the next day because I did have some phone coverage in that area, so I could call my friend if I got into trouble and she would come and get me. I finally did get some sleep but not as much as I would have liked. The best thing about the walk the next day was that I would didn't need to carry my large backpack because I wasn't planning to spend the night anywhere. I could just take my daypack with some food and plenty of water.

It was now day five, Wednesday, August 29th and the only thing that stood between me and the completion of my 1000-mile journey was a mere 21 ½ miles. I took some food and several bottles of water because I knew there was none along the way. There were no stores or restaurants along this section and it was going to be nearly 90 degrees that day. Also, the lower section of the trail does not have nearly as much shade as the upper and middle sections. It had also taken me thirty minutes to get on my socks and shoes because they were swollen and blistered, and I was in a lot of pain. When I walked out of my camper and headed very slowly to the trail behind it I prayed the whole way. When I got to the trail it was elevated about six feet higher than the road on which my camper sits so that meant I had to climb up a small but very steep hill to the trail. I just stood there and prayed for several minutes and my prayer was "Dear Lord, I know this is Your will, but do I have to do it today?" and I realized that it wouldn't be any less painful if I waited until the next day. I also started thinking about Paul again and how many miles he walked from church to church and I'm sure his feet got very sore…but then again, I'm not Paul. I said to myself I may not be Paul but I am one of God's own so I walked up the trail and headed south just keeping my eyes forward. By this time, it wasn't about the trail or about the scenery or the book, it was about the journey. I learned again that day that it wasn't about the "how" or the "what"; it was about the "why" so I kept walking. I kept my eyes forward and my focus on my goal and why I was doing it. I walked to Spring Creek and then on to Anthony and that when I had to decide whether I would call for help or continue. I had walked nine miles and only stopped a couple of times to drink some water. I had to drink a lot of water and I was already starting to use up my supply but I continued on.

By this time the pain was so extreme that I couldn't stop for long because it was very hard to get back up and going again. When I reached the 8-mile marker and that meant I had only five miles to go, I ran out of water. I didn't bring my little stove, so I couldn't boil any water and that didn't really matter because I didn't have the energy to do it anyway. (Let me say here before going on that my life was not in danger because there was a river there and I would have had some water out of it before I would die of thirst. The reason I didn't want to drink that was because I have had bacterial sickness before and it was not pretty, so I wanted to avoid it if possible.) I just kept walking. I got really hungry and I had plenty of food in my daypack, but I didn't dare eat any of it because I had no water and I could have choked on it. I needed to get my mind off my hunger and extreme thirst, so I started thinking about my childhood and remembered how on Sunday afternoons my father, my youngest sister and I would go on these long walks after church and Sunday dinner. That was one of the fondest memories of my childhood. When we took those walks it was always in the same order. My dad would always be in the front followed my baby sister and then me. I concentrated on that so hard that I felt that I could see them in front of me and that made it much easier to walk. I knew they weren't there but I concentrated on it so hard that I even talked to them about some of the things that I believed we would have discussed.

    When I reached Harpers Siding I knew that I was in a place that meant so much to my family, both good and bad. We had camped there many times when we were kids. My dad was a coal miner like many in the family and they always took vacation the last week in June and the first week of July so there may be fifty or more family members there for the entire vacation.

On this one particular vacation we had an accident, a major explosion that injured some of my cousins and my sister very badly. One cousin was burnt extremely badly. I stopped there to pray for a few minutes before I continued to walk. Again, I focused on my dad and behind him my baby sister then me. I also texted my middle sister because I had cell service down on that end of the trail and was always texted a lot. I explained my situation. She had been following my journey from the beginning so she knew what I was doing that day and she was able to give me so much support on these last few miles. She kept saying I could make it and she was praying for me. By that time, I was on the last couple of miles and I knew I would make it but at what cost? My feet were to the point that I didn't know if they would ever heal. I just kept focusing on my dad, my baby sister and me as we went down the trail.

As I was slowly approaching the 2 miles to go spot I started thinking about the next family sacred site just coming up. This site was a place that my father took me and my siblings many times when we were young. You see my father's father, my grandfather, passed away when my father was 12 years old. That was in 1935 and in the middle of the depression. My father was one of seven boys. It was such a hard time for many but especially for a single mother with a large family. They lived wherever they could and often with relatives. For part of my father's childhood they lived near

Caldwell on a hill overlooking the Greenbrier River. They spent much of their time fishing and exploring at a place they called "Naked Man's Rock". It was called that because they had a custom of skinny dipping off of that rock on New Year's Day. That was always a very special place to my father and became my favorite place. Dad would take us whenever he could get off work and we would park our car at the girl's camp and walk the mile and a half up the railroad tracks to this location and spend the day. Many times there were several family members including uncles and cousins accompanying us to this spot.

As I walked down the trail, still concentrating on following my father and my sister I was hoping that I would soon see the bench located on the trail above the sacred rock. Then I saw it and a smile came over my face. I noticed there were two bikes parked there and a pack resting on the bench, but I had to stop and sit for a moment. When I looked down at the rock that was situated on the steep incline where it stretched out into the water several feet, I noticed a man and woman with a small child swimming in the water in front of my rock. I didn't want them to be concerned that I would bother their things, so I yelled down to them that I had walked many miles and I needed to rest a moment before I went on and I would not bother their things. I told them that this was a very sacred place to me and my family and then seemingly right on cue the man said that was fine and they knew when they got here a few minutes earlier that it was a sacred place because upon their arrival they saw a beautiful majestic bald eagle sitting on the peak of this rock. I was completely and totally overwhelmed by what this stranger had told me. To me, the eagle represented my father who served his country so proudly and I knew that he was with me on my journey. I was very thankful that someone had witnessed that moment and related it to me because I was so dehydrated and drained of all my energy, I may not have seen it or even believed that I saw it. They were there to relate the story to me and to confirm the majesty of the sight. I cried the entire way the last mile and a half to my car out of respect for my father and out of thankfulness to a wonderful God that allowed me the privilege to have walked with Him and to witness the things that I witnessed.

    My life would never be the same and in a wonderful way. I made it to my car and a friend that I had known for many years was there getting her two dogs ready for a walk. I shared the story with her and then I saw another person I knew so I witnessed to all of them my joy. My five day walk I totaled 156 miles and more importantly, I had finished the task that I had so desperately wanted to do. I had finished my "Thousand Mile Journey on the Greenbrier River Trail".

CHAPTER 8

THE CONCLUSION

Over the past year I have experienced more than most people do in a lifetime. I am excited that I was able to finish this journey and am now finishing the book. The ups and downs of a truly incredible life are extremely hard to put into a few pages. It was much easier because this life I wanted you to see is through the eyes of a more mature person, thanks to the joy that I now know through the guiding hand of a gracious God. It would not have been possible to write the book before this journey because I had no idea how to put into words all the things that I had been working on for so long or the many thoughts that traveled in and out of my mind until God helped me bring it all together. God was always there but it was me that was not ready. I had not surrendered my entire consciousness to him.

Before I close this book, I want to share some of the people that helped me get to this place in my life. Of course, there is my mother that I have mentioned in this book. Now she is waiting for me in Glory! My brother joined her in 2011 as did many more members of an amazing family. I can't name them all but these two were extremely special to me.

I know I said that I would not mention names in this book, but I will mention the a few names of people who are important to me. There was one young man that wasn't family but made a place in my heart forever. This young man's name is Brady Powers Mickey. I met Brady in 2015 and although I only knew him for a short period of time, no other non-family member had such a huge impact on me over a shorter time! Brady's father worked with me at the Greenbrier Hotel and he introduced me to Brady. Brady was fifteen years old and was the youngest of four sons. He was dealing with pancreatic cancer. Pancreatic cancer usually affects older men over the age of 45. I met Brady during a time of remission and at that time that we thought maybe he had beat this horrible disease.

Brady loved life and the outdoors, and his father had introduced me to him because of my love for nature. He had been successful on a deer hunt with a bow and he was so excited. So, as a result, I made Brady a wooden plaque that included his arrow and some other outdoors items. I embedded the items in acrylic so that the plaque would last forever. In May 2015, Brady's father and I took him on a bicycle trip to my favorite place, the Cranberry backcountry for an over-night stay. It was a trip of a lifetime for Brady and even though I had made that trip so many times before, this was a trip of a lifetime for me too! You see, Brady was not just your average young man, he was special. We caught trout and I taught

Brady how to fillet them and we cooked them for him. I remember him saying he wouldn't like trout, but I don't believe that I or his father was able to have any! He always bragged how he would be the best fire builder in the group and that was true. Brady built us a beautiful and very warm fire. Brady and I spent a good bit of time talking about the business plan that I was working on and I was truly amazed of the business mind that Brady possessed. That kid was extremely smart, and we bonded over how aligned he and I were on many business philosophies and principles.

    As we biked out the second day, it was apparent that Brady was getting tired and so his father and I tried to take most of the load, but Brady continued until we got to the car. I have never and probably never will again enjoy a trip so much!

    After we returned from our trip, I designed a series of products for outdoor recreation or backpacking. I name them "Brady Packs". They will still be one of our product lines in the future. We filmed a great video about the packs on the Greenbrier River which is available on YouTube. Unfortunately, Brady had a setback and was not able to be in the video but he was in some of the still pictures and they are shown in this book. You can see in the picture with his dad wearing the packs that Brady was not well but was smiling as he always did. I was able to spend some time with Brady on his 16th birthday at the hospital and I brought him some outdoor magazines.

We lost Brady a few days later and although that has been nearly three years ago, I still have trouble writing about this wonderful young man. One of the last things Brady said to me as we were talking about this business was, "Don't mess this up". We won't Brady and you will never be forgotten! The apprentice school that is at the center of this business endeavor will be forever named "Brady Powers School of Apprenticeship Studies". Brady's middle name is Powers and what a wonderful idea that it will be powered by Brady. I will always love you Brady!

The other person that must be mentioned is my father, Denver Leslie Barker, Sr. Let me tell you just a little bit about this extraordinary man. My dad was born on January 29, 1923 in Boone County, West Virginia to Alonzo and Ethel Barker. He was one of seven brothers that were all quite striking in looks and stature. They moved to Greenbrier County, where my grandfather worked in the mining and lumber industry. My grandfather was also the deputy sheriff and drove a taxi in the Quinwood and Marfrance area. My dad's father, my grandfather, passed away in 1935 of pneumonia when my father was just 12 years old. The Great Depression was an extremely hard time for the family, as my grandmother was in the position of head of household for their family. Dad always said that they could hear her crying into the late hours of the night. You could never find a group of men with such a deep love of their mother other than the Barker boys. She was adored by all that knew her.

After the passing of his father, my dad struggled to get through school because all the boys, including Dad, had to work every minute they could just so the family could survive. At 17, my father and a friend decided to lie about their ages and joined the Civil Conservation Corps (CCC) so that they could bring more money to the family. Dad always said that he and his friend believed that they would be sent to the local area because there were CCC camps locally. My dad's friend became a member of the local units, but my father was sent to the state of Oregon to work. Dad said he was so afraid on that train because they had let many bad elements, even prisoners, go to these camps. He went on to Oregon where he worked hard building fences and planting trees. He also finished his 9th grade in school during that time. Dad was paid $29 a month with $22 being sent home to his mother each month. That left him $7 but they furnished everything for them. He was happy to help the family.

From there he came home and worked for a bit and then World War II began, and he joined the army, where he served until the end of the war. My father was one of the brave soldiers that went on shore on Omaha Beach in France on D-Day. He was in the Second Wave, as he and many others waited in transports out in the English Channel for their time to go onshore. Rough seas and loud blasts of cannon fire and storm conditions were constant, but he endured until his turn. When he got onshore, there were so many dead. There was still fire from the German guns and our ships had started firing over their heads to the enemy positions. I can't even imagine what those soldiers endured but they did it so that we could remain a free nation! My father made it on shore and into the French countryside until he was wounded in the Hedgerow part of France where they were battling Hitler's Elite Tank Division. He was sent to a hospital in London and finished out his time at an Airforce base there.

    My father returned home. His mother didn't even know that he was discharged until he knocked on the door! He thought that he would get some time off, but the local coal mines called him the next day and he went to work in an industry in which he would proudly spend 43 years. My mother and my father were married 57 years and they raised five children. I am so very proud to a part of this family! My father and mother were saved in a revival not long after they were married and we were all raised in a God-fearing home, of which today I am so thankful. In the first chapter I talked extensively about the early years of my life and how much I enjoyed it. I was always thankful for my parents!

    I could write several books about my father, but fast forward to this book and my father's impact on me in the past several years. When my mother passed away it was really hard on my father, as you would expect. They were married for 57 years and now my father was alone because all of his children, including me, lived out of state. After a few years, I decided to move back to the Greenbrier County area to be close to dad. He was still very independent and liked living alone but he also liked someone living in the area. I lived in the little camp that we had for many years in Renick, WV, then eventually I moved into the house in Rainelle with him. I was still single from my second divorce in 2000 and I was the best choice of five siblings there to keep an eye on him. I had no problem with that, because it was to be close to the man I loved most in this world and to the place I loved more than any other place. I was able to spend eight years with him and truly enjoyed every minute and I believe he did, also. He used to say nearly every day that we have such a wonderful life. He was and still is adored by all his children, grandchildren and great-grandchildren.

    I don't feel that it is appropriate to write all the details, but we lost our father on June 24, 2016 in the devastating flood that hit West Virginia. It hit Greenbrier County especially hard! I found my amazing father that morning in the living room floor of his home. He was 93 years old and still in good health and his mind was incredible. I could go on forever about him and I couldn't tell half of his great attributes. The only thing that I will relate to you is that the walk that morning to the house where he lived was one of my hardest. It wasn't because I was wading in waist deep, dirty, filthy cold water but more because I knew what was ahead. We all had thought that he was rescued the night before. I could not get to him for all of the high water everywhere. I only learned just a few minutes before that he didn't make it out of the house. I was trying to prepare myself for what I was about to see. It was hard, but I wanted it to be me and I wanted to do it alone.

    I walked up the steps to the house where my mother had passed away and now, my father. The main door was open and I could see my dad lying on the floor face down with his feet against the screen door. The mud and water were still a couple inches deep and when I walked in the first things I noticed was that mom's picture had floated to his side and that the flashlight I had bought him the day before was still in his hand. All the furniture was turned over and the house was a real mess because there had been over four feet of water in the house that day and the night before. I'll never forget as long as I live the next few minutes. I got down in that muddy water and put my arm around my father and we talked for probably 15 or 20 minutes. I remember telling him, "I will get you out of here", but I didn't know how. I left the house and walked down to the corner and met the Sheriff of Greenbrier County and I knew that he loved my dad very much. With all he had going on that day, he had shown up and corralled three National Guard members and after a long hug he told those other gentlemen that this man was a war hero and he wouldn't stay in that water any longer. He then told me to go on that he would take care of him and he did. He is truly our family's hero.

I struggled a long time after this because I missed Dad so much but also because I blamed myself and others for his death. My dad died on my watch and I felt responsible and no one could convince me otherwise. I had also lost everything that I owned and even the home that I lived in. I'm still working to rebuild that life. My cousin from Arkansas brought me his camper to live in while I was rebuilding the house in which Dad and I lived. As I have tried so hard in this book to explain; in the past year my life has gone through a dramatic change. I no longer blame anyone else, not even myself.

Within the pages of this book I have explained in detail the experience, education and passion presented to you in this *action* plan. The part that I must have you to understand is that until this tragic event, I really did not completely understand what people go through in these types of disasters. I now do. If I can help one person that lost everything or one veteran or one person fighting drug abuse it will all be worth it. That's my "**WHY**"!

Please visit our website to find out more details about this plan and to establish contact with us: www.fourthteeliving.com

COMING IN 2019

MY FINAL THOUSAND MILE JOURNEY

This will be the second in a series of books that this author will be releasing later in the year. "My Final Thousand Mile Journey" will be released around Easter 2019. The first book of this series gave the readers a look into the author's past life and experiences along with his vision for a future world. The first book was how the pieces of the puzzle came together and the beginning to putting the puzzle together. The second book of this series is a book of fiction that will show the picture on the front of the box. "My Final Thousand Mile Journey" is a clear vision into the future that will show the possibilities that can be obtained.

MY DREAM HOME

Throughout the first book in this series and the main theme of the second book is a home design that is the central part of this vision. This book will detail in every way the building of this the fourth and most complete design. Every part of this project from start to finish will be chronicled in this book. From drawings to application for construction permits will be included. We will also include every step of the process including all costs associated from foundation to move-in. This book will give the reader the possibility to build their own dream home in their own time.

MY SECOND THOUSAND MILE JOURNEY

This will be the fourth book of the series and will be much like the first book of this series. The author will embark on his second thousand-mile journey and his travels will be included, much like the first book. Also, all efforts and movements toward the continued assembly of puzzle pieces towards the picture on the front of the box will be included.

Made in the USA
Columbia, SC
30 March 2019